The media's watching Vault!
Here's a sampling of our coverage.

"For those hoping to climb the ladder of success, [Vault's] insights are priceless."
– *Money magazine*

"The best place on the web to prepare for a job search."
– *Fortune*

"[Vault guides] make for excellent starting points for job hunters and should be purchased by academic libraries for their career sections [and] university career centers."
– *Library Journal*

"The granddaddy of worker sites."
– *U.S. News & World Report*

"A killer app."
– *New York Times*

D1530792

One of Forbes' 33 "Favorite Sites"
– *Forbes*

"To get the unvarnished scoop, check out Vault."
– *SmartMoney Magazine*

"Vault has a wealth of information about major employers and job-searching strategies as well as comments from workers about their experiences at specific companies."
– *The Washington Post*

"A key reference for those who want to know what it takes to get hired by a law firm and what to expect once they get there."
– *New York Law Journal*

"Vault [provides] the skinny on working conditions at all kinds of companies from current and former employees."
– *USA Today*

> the most trusted name in career information™

VAULT GUIDE TO
FINANCE INTERVIEWS

VAULT GUIDE TO
FINANCE INTERVIEWS

D. BHATAWEDEKHAR, DAN JACOBSON,
HUSSAM HAMADEH
AND THE STAFF OF VAULT

ACKNOWLEDGMENTS

We are extremely grateful to Vault's entire staff for all their help in the editorial, production and marketing processes. Vault also would like to acknowledge the support of our investors, clients, employees, family, and friends. Thank you!

Table of Contents

MERGERS & ACQUISITIONS 121

BRAINTEASERS AND GUESSTIMATES 133

FINAL ANALYSIS 147

APPENDIX 149

Visit the Vault Finance Career Channel at **www.vault.com/finance** — with
insider firm profiles, message boards, the Vault Finance Job Board and more.

VAULT CAREER LIBRARY

xi

Decrease your T/NJ Ratio
(Time to New Job)

Use the Internet's most targeted job search tools for finance professionals.

Vault Finance Job Board

The most comprehensive and convenient job board for finance professionals. Target your search by area of finance, function, and experience level, and find the job openings that you want. No surfing required.

VaultMatch Resume Database

Vault takes match-making to the next level: post your resume and customize your search by area of finance, experience and more. We'll match job listings with your interests and criteria and e-mail them directly to your inbox.

VAULT
> the most trusted name in career information™

INTRODUCTION

Landing a Gig

Money makes the world go round, and those in charge of money are the financiers. Have thirst for relevance? The finance industry has always been a competitive field, due in large part to the glamour and prestige assigned to the working relationships with industry titans. Of course, the outstanding salaries explain much of the pull as well. (Unless you can dunk a basketball or throw football 50 yards, it's hard to beat the pay in investment banking, where recent college grads can come close to six figures.)

So what's the secret to landing a finance gig? Naturally, identifying opportunities is the first step. Many finance firms have structured on-campus recruiting processes. If you're in college or graduate school (especially business school), check with the career services office to see which finance companies recruit at your campus. If the company you've got your eye on doesn't come to your school, don't despair. Many firms accept resumes from non-targeted schools. Check the firm's web site to find out how to submit your resume. Firm web sites are also a good bet for those out of school looking to change jobs or careers. Additionally, check with friends and alumni for openings at a specific firm or in the finance industry in general.

Virtually every recruiter or professional agrees that no matter how you hear about your position, the most important factor in getting a job is making a good impression in your interview. No matter what your credentials, experience or references, if you don't come off in your interviews as someone who can do the job and who will fit in at the company, you stand little to no chance of getting hired.

Don't be too put off by the pressure. If you've landed an initial interview, you can assume someone at the firm, in reviewing your resume, thinks you've got at least the basics necessary to succeed. It's now up to you to prove that to your interviewers by being confident and knowledgeable. This guide will familiarize you with the questions you're likely to receive in the course of your interview. As you'll see, you can expect to tested to make sure you can work under pressure, fit into the company's culture and excel in your job.

Finance career opportunities can be broadly divided into several categories, most prominently investment banking, commercial banking, asset management, venture capital and private equity, and finance positions at a corporation like Dell or The Coca-Cola Company (also referred to as "corporate finance"). There is considerable movement between these positions — I-bankers leave to take posts in industry, or with private equity firms, etc. Generally, the pinnacle for most finance professionals is either as a partner or managing director of a bank, a portfolio manager for an asset management firm, or as Chief Financial Officer (CFO) of a company. The interviews for each of these industries are very similar.

For more information on finance interviews and finance careers, go to the Vault Finance Career Channel

- Employer surveys on hundreds of top finance employers

- The *Vault Guide to Advanced and Quantitative Finance Interviews* and the *Vault Finance Interviews Practice Guide*

- Thousands of top finance jobs on the Vault Finance Job Board

- Finance Resume Review and Writing – named the "Top Choice" for resume makeovers by *The Wall Street Journal*

- One-on-one finance interview prep with Vault finance interview experts

- The *Vault Guide to the Top 50 Banking Employers*, the *Vault Career Guide to Investment Banking*, the *Vault Career Guide to Hedge Funds*, the *Vault Career Guide to Investment Management*, and other Vault finance guides

www.vault.com/finance

Visit the Vault Finance Career Channel at **www.vault.com/finance** — with insider firm profiles, message boards, the Vault Finance Job Board and more.

V∧ULT CAREER LIBRARY

3

THE FINANCIAL
SERVICES
INDUSTRY

The Finance Interview: An Overview

Investment banking and other finance positions are among the most stressful and demanding positions on the planet and interviews in finance often test an applicant's tolerance for such an environment. To test an applicant's stamina, interviews in finance traditionally involve three or four rounds at a minimum, and each round may have up to six interviews, with the number of interviews generally increasing in each round. To test an applicant's ability to handle stress, interviewers may adopt aversive or stressful interviewing tactics. Insiders say that occasionally a bank or finance interviewer will go so far as to use techniques from rapid-fire quantitative questions such as "How many planes are currently flying over the United States right now?" to confrontational questions such as, "Why should I give you this job? Your resume doesn't fit our profile." Firms may ask you specific and detailed questions about your grades in college or business school, even if your school policy prohibits such questions. At other firms, interview rounds may be interspersed with seemingly casual and friendly dinners. Don't let down your guard! While these dinners are a good opportunity to meet your prospective co-workers, your seemingly genial hosts are scrutinizing you as well. (Read: Don't drink too much.)

There are generally two parts to the finance hiring process: the "fit part" and the "technical part." The "fit part" is where the hiring firm deciphers whether or not you fit into their group's culture. The "technical part" is where the interviewer judges your analytical and technical skills. If you don't know the basic concepts of finance and accounting, your interviewers will believe (rightly) that you are either 1) not interested in the position or 2) not competent enough to handle the job. While a good deal of this book is devoted to helping you ace the technical part of finance interviews, it is arguably more important that you nail the fit interview, proving that you are someone the people in the group would like to work with. As you go through recruiting in finance interviews, understand that you compete with yourself. Most firms are flexible enough to hire people that are a good fit.

The fit interview

They call it the O'Hare airport test, the Atlanta airport test, or the whatever-city-you-happen-to-be-applying-in airport test. They also call it the fit interview or the behavioral interview. It means: "Could you stand to be stranded in an airport for eight hours with this person?"

Generally, while your performance in the fit interview partly depends – as the airport test suggests – on your personality fit, it also depends on your "career fit," or your ability to portray yourself as a good fit as an investment banker, asset manager, and so on. In other words, interviewers will try to figure out what your attitude towards work is like, how interested you are in a career in the industry, and how interested you are in the job for which you are applying.

I'm a hard worker

As a general rule, you should emphasize how hard you have worked in the past, giving evidence of your ability to take on a lot of work and pain. You don't have to make things up or pretend that there's nothing you'd want more than to work 100-hour weeks. In fact, interviewers are sure to see through such blatant lying. Says one I-banking interviewer, "If somebody acted too enthusiastic about the hours, that'd be weird." If you ask investment bankers and others in finance what they dislike most about their jobs, they will most likely talk about the long hours. Be honest about this unpleasant part of the job, and convince your interviewer that you can handle it well. For example, if you were in crew and had to wake up at five every morning in the freezing cold, by all means, talk about it. If you put yourself through school by working two jobs, mention that, too. And if no experience applies, at least acknowledge the hours as a necessary part of a career path you are choosing.

Got safe hands?

As with all job interviews, finance interviews will be focused on figuring out whether you can handle the responsibility required of the position, understandable considering that in many cases with finance positions, that responsibility may mean making decisions with millions or billions of dollars.

An interviewer will try and figure out if you've got safe hands and won't be dropping the ball. "This is a critical I-banking concept," says one banker about safe hands. "The idea is: 'Can I give this person this analysis to do and feel comfortable that they will execute it promptly and correctly?' The people with safe hands are the ones who advance in the company. They are not necessarily the hardest workers but they are the most competent." Make sure you bring up examples of taking responsibility and getting complex, detail-oriented jobs done right.

Visit the Vault Finance Career Channel at **hwww.vault.com/finance** — with insider firm profiles, message boards, the Vault Finance Job Board and more.

VAULT CAREER LIBRARY

7

A mind to pick things apart

The world of finance involves a lot of number crunching and analytical ability. And while you don't have to be a world-class mathematician, you do have to have an analytic mind if you are going to succeed. Explains one insider at a numbers-heavy Wall Street firm, "you can't be any old English major. You've got to have a really logical, mathematical head." Make sure you have examples of your problem-solving and analytic strengths, particularly those involving quantitative analysis.

T-E-A-M! Go team!

Teamwork is a popular buzzword for employers of all industries. Every finance position (except, perhaps, for research) requires that an employee work closely with others – whether in investment banking deal teams or in cross-fuctional corporate teams such as the finance officials working with marketers at a large corporation. Interviewers will ask questions to make sure that you have experience and have excelled in team situations. Sure, you can break out those glory days stories about the winning touchdown pass, but hopefully there are more poignant situations which can also help describe your teamwork ability – previous work experience, volunteer activities, or school work in teams, to name a few.

Preparing for finance interviews

When you review career options, don't discount the amount of time it takes to prepare for finance interviews. First of all, you should evaluate whether you actually want to be in finance. In short, you should know what you're getting into. Not only should you know this for your own sake (this is your future, after all), but your interviewers want to know that you understand the position and industry.

You should use the opportunity of non-evaluative settings (i.e., not an interview) to ascertain if finance is for you. These are questions to which we strongly suggest you have answers to before interviewing. Make a point to attend recruiting presentations by firms. Informational interviews with alumni and (for those in business school) second-years are also good ways to get answers to some of your questions.

As for written materials, you can start with general business publications like *The Wall Street Journal*, *The Economist*, *BusinessWeek*, and the *Financial Times*. From there, you can move on to trade publications that will give more industry-specific news and analysis. *American Banker*,

Institutional Investor, *Investment Dealers' Digest* and *The Daily Deal* are some examples.

Your interaction with alumni can have direct results. The results can be good if you prepare properly before contacting them, are sufficiently informed, ask good and sincere questions, and show proper respect. You can also assure yourself a ding if you don't handle a meeting or phone conversation correctly.

Here are some questions about finance positions you should ask before you have your first interview:

• What is a typical day like?

• What are the hours in the industry really like? Are they 100 hours every week or every other week? Is it the same for every firm?

• How do people cope with the lifestyle issues in the industry?

• What kind of money do people make in the industry?

• What are the things I-bankers (or commercial bankers, venture capitalists, etc.) like about their jobs? What would they like to change?

• What is the future of the industry for the next few years? How will the industry change? How will the margins change? The return on equity?

• What is the career track in the industry? What skills are required at what stage?

• What is so exciting about this job?

• What is the culture of an I-banking firm as compared to a Fortune 500 company? Compared to a startup?

• What are the exit opportunities after 10 years in the industry? After two years?

Research individual firms

Once you've answered questions about the industry, you should begin to narrow your research to specific firms – both to know which firms to target, and to be knowledgeable for your interviews. Good sources for research are easily accessible publications like *The Wall Street Journal*, *BusinessWeek* and *Fortune*. If you have the resources (perhaps at a school library), you can also read through recent issues of trade publications like *Investment Dealers' Digest*. And of course, to get the inside scoop on culture, pay, and hiring at top firms, read the company profiles on www.vault.com, as well as guides like *The Vault Guide to the Top 50 Banking Employers* and *The Vault Guide to the Top Financial Services Firms*.

Insiders at business school who have gone through the recruiting process suggest that you form research and interview practice teams. There is a lot of material to cover, and it is not possible to do it all by yourself. Form teams for researching industries and firms. Later, you can use the same teams to practice interviews. If you are an undergraduate, you should try to see if your school has an investment banking or finance club. If you are in business school, your school will undoubtedly have such a club, or you may want to team up with other students who are looking into finance careers. Teams of four to six work quite well for this research process.

Practice your interviews

As you read this guide, you should prepare answers to common questions given at finance interviews – whether they be fit questions, technical questions, or brainteasers. While this may be easiest for technical questions and brainteasers (after all, we can help you to nail those questions with the right answers), it is also important to prepare for fit questions even if there are no right or wrong answers. We can steer you onto the right path with these questions, but you'll need to fill in the blanks. What's the hardest thing you've ever had to do? Can you give me an example of a time when you came up with a creative solution? You don't want to be cursing yourself after an interview, thinking about what you should have said, or examples you could have brought up.

One of the best ways to prepare answers to these questions is to use mock/practice interviews. You can practice by role-playing with your friends and classmates, or by taking advantage of interview training offered by your school. Most MBA career centers, and many undergraduate career centers, offer students the opportunity to perform mock interviews, which are normally videotaped. These practice sessions are conducted either by professional career counselors or by second-year students. The mock interviewees are given the videotape of their critique to watch at home (again and again). Students may choose what kind of interview they'd like to receive: finance, consulting, etc.

What mistakes are commonly unearthed by the videotaped interview? One business school career counselor says that he finds that "most MBAs don't have their story down. They can't elaborate on why they came to business school, and why they want to work in the industry." The best candidates are able to describe their background and career history, and make a pitch about why they are interested in a firm, all in a minute or less, career counselors say. Another problem is that many students apparently "can't elaborate their strengths. They have them, but can't sell them. They are too modest." While there's no use demurring when explicating your good points, career center professionals warn that "there is also a danger of tooting your horn too much" – so make sure you're not making any claims for competency you can't back up with relevant experience.

To take full advantage of their mock interviews, career counselors say, you should take them as seriously as possible. Dress professionally "to get into the interviewing mindset." Afterwards, the interviewer will go over the session, assessing your strengths and weaknesses. It's a good idea to take notes on this feedback.

Mock interviewers also coach students on appropriate answers. "For example," explains one mock interviewer, "many candidates are asked to name their top three weaknesses. Answering with your actual weaknesses is not a good idea. So when I identify a student's weaker point – maybe they are weak on real teamwork experience – we strategize on an appropriate answer. It's better to say something like 'I wouldn't call them weaknesses, but there are three areas in which I still have room to grow,' and then choose three areas that are not deal-breakers."

Do interviewers thus end up hearing the same canned answers over and over again? "I do hear from some interviewers at certain schools – not mine! – that they do hear identical answers to certain questions," says one insider. "My advice to students is to always put answers into their own words."

Prepare questions

Finally, don't forget that finance interviewers often ask candidates whether they have any questions. Don't get caught looking like a job applicant who hasn't done research and is not curious about the opportunities. Read about the firms, read about the industries, and prepare some intelligent questions. Also, remember that, when in doubt, you can allow the interviewers to talk about themselves with questions like, "Tell me about your career path" and "Describe your typical day-to-day responsibilities."

Visit the Vault Finance Career Channel at hwww.vault.com/finance — with insider firm profiles, message boards, the Vault Finance Job Board and more.

VAULT CAREER LIBRARY   11

Questions

1. Why do you want to do investment banking/investment management/ whatever career you plan to pursue?

This is a question you are almost guaranteed to receive. First and foremost, you must emphasize that you know what the finance department in which you are interviewing does. Talk to as many people in the industry before the interview to get a good idea of the job function's day-to-day tasks as well as the general description of the work a person in that job is asked to perform. Then, when asked the question, you need not state that you've yearned to be in finance your life, but you should illustrate succinctly that you know the job functions of the position for which you are interviewing, that you enjoy performing these functions, and that you have developed the core skills required (i.e., analytical ability, good communication skills, and, of course, a strong work ethic and willingness to put in the hours to do the job).

2. What exactly do investment bankers (or investment managers, etc.) do?

Don't laugh. You'd be astonished at how many people go to interview with Goldman Sachs or Fidelity Investments without having a clear idea of what they'll be doing if they actually get the job. You are very likely to receive this question if you are a career-changer or if you have a non-financial background. You'd better know the basics of your industry – for example, that investment bankers raise capital for companies in the public or private marketplace or that investment managers manage money for individuals and institutions.

3. Here's a whiteboard. Stand in front of it and present a chapter from your favorite finance textbook. You have five minutes.

May we suggest not selecting the introduction? The point of this question is twofold. First of all, the interviewers want to test your ability to explain complicated financial matters in lucid terms. Secondly, they want to test your on-the-spot presentation skills. Practice with a friend – even with your professor, if you can – until you're comfortable presenting this material.

4. Walk me through your resume.

Again, highlight those activities and previous positions that are most applicable to the core finance skills. Also talk about the things you are proud of and that set you apart. Finally, illustrate that your educational and career moves follow a logical sequence.

5. Let me give you a situation: It is Friday afternoon. Tomorrow morning you have to catch a flight to Boston for your best friend's marriage, and you are in the wedding. You have informed your deal team well in advance and they know that you will be gone. Just when you are about to leave, you find out that a client wants to meet with the banking team tomorrow. What will you do?

One of the big assets you bring to a finance position, especially those with investment banks, is your attitude towards work. This is a rather tricky question, but use this to express the fact that you understand the hardships that an I-banking career would involve, and that you have endured such sacrifice situations previously.

6. Say you are supposed to meet your girlfriend for dinner but the MD asks you to stay late. What do you do? Can you give me an example of a similar situation you have faced before?

Another attitude question. Be prepared.

7. Why should we hire you?

When answering an open-ended question like this, try to make them insightful and entertaining like you did for your school applications. Again, this question begs you to illustrate that you understand the position for which you are interviewing and that you are hardworking, analytical, and team-oriented. Prepare examples and as you do, think of them as if they were speeches. What would your stories and anecdotes be? Would they be exciting? Funny? Insightful? Absorbing? Something that the audience would remember for a long time? Unique?

8. Why did you decide to do an MBA?

If you are an MBA student looking for a finance position, you are probably going to get this question. If you came from a finance background, you can talk about how you thought you would add to your skill set by going to business school, and how that expectation has panned out. If you did not, simply answer the question as honestly as you can. As an aside, it is perfectly appropriate to respond that you are getting an MBA as a means for changing careers.

9. What types of activities did you pursue while in college?

While it may be all good and well to talk about the soup kitchen, remember that you're interviewing for intense, stressful positions. Says one interviewer, "We love to see people who worked part-time, went to all six of their classes, got As and don't seem to need sleep. Frankly, banks like people in debt who will kill themselves for the big bonus. I believe 'hungry' people are highly valued in the interview process."

10. Why are you applying to this firm?

Do your research and find out what each firm prides itself on, whether it be international presence, team-orientation or social environment. Get ready to talk about the industry and the firm specifically. For some firms (smaller, specialized I-banks like Lazard, for example), this is an especially important question. Says one insider at a boutique firm, "You definitely want to have someone who knows what they're getting into. I don't think its advisable to say I'm looking at all the bulge-bracket firms – plus [yours]. You want to see people who are very focused." And even at those big firms that all seem the same, your interviewer will be impressed and flattered if you can talk about how his or her firm is different and why that interests you.

11. Give me an example of a project that you've done that involved heavy analytical thinking.

Candidates without a financial background should have an answer prepared for this question that describes a work or school project, focusing on the part that required a lot of number crunching.

12. If you were the CEO of our bank, what three things would change?

An interesting question. This question assumes, first of all, that you've done enough research on your potential future employer to answer this question. Telling your interviewers that you'd open an office in Shanghai may be a good answer – but not if the firm already has an office in that city. Be prepared to defend your answers. Avoid being too negative – "I'd fire the CFO" is a bad answer if one of your interviewers works with him.

13. What is your favorite web site?

Up to you. If you own stock, it's fine to choose a site like Ameritrade. You could choose Vault, for the research on your favorite firms. If you want to impress them with your business savvy, you could simply choose a web site that you think is run especially well, like eBay. Just be prepared to back up your answer with specific information.

14. Tell me about the stock price of a company in your prior line of work.

Make sure you're conversant with how your previous employers (or competitors) are doing before you interview.

15. Give me an example of a time you worked as part of a team.

You're sure to get this one. Draw on experiences from previous work experience, from volunteer activities, and from any other situation in which you worked with others toward a common goal. Highlight your strengths as a team member: empathy, collaboration and consensus-building are good themes to emphasize.

16. What is the most striking thing you've read recently in *The Wall Street Journal*?

A variation of this question is: "What publications do you read regularly?" With these questions, your interviews want to see how well read you are, how interested you are in finance, and how well you can describe any of the recent burning financial issues. Read the *Journal* regularly, especially when it is close to the interview time. We suggest starting with 45 minutes a day and gradually bringing that down as you become more efficient in your information-gathering.

17. Describe a project you have worked on that you enjoyed.

Yet another opportunity to show that you are a hardworking, responsible, analytical team player.

18. Let's say I give you this summer job/full-time job today. Now let's move to the future and say that at the end of the summer, you find out that you did not get a full-time offer, or that six months into the job you are fired. Give me three reasons why this could happen, and what you can do to prevent this.

This is a twist on the "what are your biggest weaknesses" question, made specifically more stressful for the finance interview. Don't lose your cool, and have answers prepared.

Visit the Vault Finance Career Channel at hwww.vault.com/finance — with insider firm profiles, message boards, the Vault Finance Job Board and more.

VAULT CAREER LIBRARY   **15**

19. Think of a person you feel knows you very well both professionally and socially. If I were to call this person and ask him to describe you, what would he say?

Yet another version of the strengths and weaknesses question.

20. What motivates you?

Think through this one. First of all, you should indicate that you are highly motivated. Second, remember the profile that finance interviews are generally looking for. Appropriate answers include financial security, problem-solving, deadlines, and productivity. Again, be prepared to give examples.

21. Can you give me an example of an experience of failure?

You should have an answer prepared for this question. Be modest and admit that you have experienced setbacks. Also, focus on how you bounced back from the setback and what you learned from the experience.

22. You don't seem like you are a very driven person. How will you be able to handle a job in banking?

A stress question that can easily hit you at the tail end of a long and tiring interview process. After meeting with more than a dozen people in a day, it may be very easy to appear worn out, which is precisely what you must avoid – you must convince your interviewer that you don't wear out easily by displaying good energy. Come up with good examples of a time when you were totally driven despite fatiguing circumstances.

23. Tell me about an accomplishment that you are proud of.

This is your chance to shine. Remember: team-oriented, analytical, hardworking, dependable.

24. What was your favorite course in school? Your least favorite? Why? What were your grades in each?

Have a few choices ready and be prepared to justify them. Don't say that you didn't like a class because it was "too hard" or "had too much math" or even that "the professor was unreasonable" (because your interviewer may wonder if you'll think your boss unreasonable as well). Remember that your interviewer most likely has your transcript in front of her, so don't try to inflate your grades.

25. Tell me how you have modeled with equations in the past.

If you're an economics major, or if you've owned a business, you shouldn't have a problem answering this question. Even if you're a non-finance major, you should have at least one class or real-life example you can provide. If you've never done financial modeling, do at least one example before the interview or have someone walk you through the process.

26. Who have you talked to at our bank?

This is actually a good sign – your interviewer may ask them for impressions of you. You should remember the names of any representatives who have attended campus career events. Hopefully, in your research you've connected with people at that firm.

27. Can you tell me about a time when you handled many things at the same time?

In some finance positions, especially I-banking, multi-tasking is an important attribute. Think through your background and prepare for this question.

28. What would you like for me to tell you?

Remember, you will be asked if you have any questions. Do your research and impress your interviewer with your knowledge and insight. However, don't ask transparent questions that seem like you are only asking them because you have to. And, again, when in doubt, ask about their own personal experiences.

29. What is a hedge fund?

This is obviously a popular question for those candidates interviewing for the increasingly popular and prestigious hedge fund positions. Surprisingly, many candidates have no feel for what distinguishes a hedge fund from other types of funds.

A hedge fund is a private investment partnership which uses aggressive strategies unavailable to other types of funds, most popularly mutual funds. Hedge funds are required by law to have less than 100 investors, and liberally use such financial techniques and vehicles as short-selling, swaps, risk arbitrage and derivatives Since they are restricted by law to less than 100 investors, the minimum hedge-fund investment is typically $1 million. (For more information, get the *Vault Career Guide to Hedge Funds*.)

Decrease your T/NJ Ratio
(Time to New Job)

Use the Internet's most targeted job search tools for finance professionals.

Vault Finance Job Board

The most comprehensive and convenient job board for finance professionals. Target your search by area of finance, function, and experience level, and find the job openings that you want. No surfing required.

VaultMatch Resume Database

Vault takes match-making to the next level: post your resume and customize your search by area of finance, experience and more. We'll match job listings with your interests and criteria and e-mail them directly to your inbox.

VALUATION TECHNIQUES

How Much is it Worth?

Imagine yourself as the CEO of a publicly traded company that makes widgets. You've had a highly successful business so far and want to sell the company to anyone interested in buying it. How do you know how much to sell it for? Likewise, consider the Bank of America acquisition of Fleet. How did B of A decide how much it should pay to buy Fleet?

For starters, you should understand that the value of a company is equal to the value of its assets, and that

$$\text{Value of Assets} = \text{Debt} + \text{Equity}$$

or

$$\text{Assets} = D + E$$

If I buy a company, I buy its stock (equity) and assume its debt (bonds and loans). Buying a company's equity means that I actually gain ownership of the company – if I buy 50 percent of a company's equity, I own 50 percent of the company. Assuming a company's debt means that I promise to pay the company's lenders the amount owed by the previous owner.

The value of debt is easy to calculate: the market value of debt is equal to the book value of debt. (Unless the debt trades and thus has a real "market value." This information, however, is hard to come by, so it is safe to use the book value.) Figuring out the market value of equity is trickier, and that's where valuation techniques come into play.

The four most commonly used techniques are:

1. Discounted cash flow (DCF) analysis
2. Multiples method
3. Market valuation
4. Comparable transactions method

Generally, before we can understand valuation, we need to understand accounting, the language upon which valuation is based.

Basic Accounting Concepts

Before we look at these valuation techniques, let's take a look at basic accounting concepts that underpin valuation. MBAs interested in finance careers should definitely be comfortable with these concepts (and may find this overview to be very basic). Undergrads who have taken accounting classes should already be familiar with these concepts as well.

Basic overview of financial statements

There are four basic financial statements that provide the information you need to evaluate a company:

- Balance Sheets
- Income Statements
- Statements of Cash Flows
- Statements of Retained Earnings

These four statements are provided in the annual reports (also referred to as "10Ks") published by public companies. In addition, a company's annual report is almost always accompanied by notes to the financial statements. These notes provide additional information about each line item of numbers provided in the four basic financial statements.

The Balance Sheet

The Balance Sheet presents the financial position of a company at a given point in time. It is comprised of three parts: Assets, Liabilities, and Shareholder's Equity. Assets are the economic resources of a company. They are the resources that the company uses to operate its business and include Cash, Inventory, and Equipment. (Both financial statements and accounts in financial statements are capitalized.) A company normally obtains the resources it uses to operate its business by incurring debt, obtaining new investors, or through operating earnings. The Liabilities section of the Balance Sheet presents the debts of the company. Liabilities are the claims that creditors have on the company's resources. The Equity section of the Balance Sheet presents the net worth of a company, which equals the assets that the company owns less the debts it owes to creditors. In other words, equity is comprised of the claims that investors have on the company's resources after debt is paid off.

The most important equation to remember is that

Assets (A) = Liabilities (L) + Shareholder's Equity (SE)

The structure of the Balance Sheet is based on that equation.

This example uses the basic format of a Balance Sheet:

Media Entertainment, Inc			
Balance Sheet			
(December 31, 2005)			
Assets		**Liabilities**	
Cash	203,000	Accounts Payable	7,000
Accounts Receivable	26,000		
Building	19,000	**Equity**	
		Common Stock	10,000
		Retained Earnings	231,000
Total Assets	248,000	**Total Liabilities & Equity**	248,000

With respect to the right side of the balance sheet, because companies can obtain resources from both investors and creditors, they must distinguish between the two. Companies incur debt to obtain the economic resources necessary to operate their businesses and promise to pay the debt back over a specified period of time. This promise to pay is based on a fixed payment schedule and is not based upon the operating performance of the company. Companies also seek new investors to obtain economic resources. However, they don't promise to pay investors back a specified amount over a specified period of time. Instead, companies forecast for a return on their investment that is often contingent upon assumptions the company or investor makes about the level of operating performance. Since an equity holder's investment is not guaranteed, it is more risky in nature than a loan made by a creditor. If a company performs well, the upside to investors is higher. The promise-to-pay element makes loans made by creditors a Liability and, as an accountant would say, more "senior" than equity holdings, as it is paid back before distributions to equity-holders are made.

To summarize, the Balance Sheet represents the economic resources of a business. One side includes assets, the other includes liabilites (debt) and shareholder's equity, and Assets = L+E. On the liability side, debts owed to creditors are more senior than the investments of equity holders and are classified as Liabilities, while equity investments are accounted for in the Equity section of the Balance Sheet.

The Income Statement

We have discussed two of the three ways in which a company normally obtains the economic resources necessary to operate its business: incurring debt and seeking new investors. A third way in which a company can obtain resources is through its own operations. The Income Statement presents the results of operations of a business over a specified period of time (e.g., one year, one quarter, one month) and is composed of Revenues, Expenses and Net Income.

Revenue: Revenue is a source of income that normally arises from the sale of goods or services and is recorded when it is earned. For example, when a retailer of roller blades makes a sale, the sale would be considered revenue.

Expenses: Expenses are the costs incurred by a business over a specified period of time to generate the revenues earned during that same period of time. For example, in order for a manufacturing company to sell a product, it must buy the materials it needs to make the product. In addition, that same company must pay people to both make and sell the product. The company must also pay salaries to the individuals who operate the business. These are all types of expenses that a company can incur during the normal operations of the business. When a company incurs an expense outside of its normal operations, it is considered a loss. Losses are expenses incurred as a result of one-time or incidental transactions. The destruction of office equipment in a fire, for example, would be a loss.

Assets and expenses

Incurring expenses and acquiring assets both involve the use of economic resources (i.e., cash or debt). So, when is a purchase considered an asset and when is it considered an expense?

Assets vs. expenses: A purchase is considered an asset if it provides future economic benefit to the company, while expenses only relate to the current period. For example, monthly salaries paid to employees for services they already provided to the company would be considered expenses. On the other hand, the purchase of a piece of manufacturing equipment would be classified as an asset, as it will probably be used to manufacture a product for more than one accounting period.

Visit the Vault Finance Career Channel at **www.vault.com/finance** — with insider firm profiles, message boards, the Vault Finance Job Board and more.

VAULT CAREER LIBRARY   23

Net income: The Revenue a company earns, less its Expenses over a specified period of time, equals its Net Income. A positive Net Income number indicates a profit, while a negative Net Income number indicates that a company suffered a loss (called a "net loss").

Here is an example of an Income Statement:

Media Entertainment, Inc
Income Statement
(For the year ended December 31, 2005)

Revenues		
Services Billed		100,000
Expenses		
Salaries and Wages	(33,000)	
Rent Expense	(17,000)	
Utilities Expense	(7,000)	(57,000)
Net Income		43,000

To summarize, the Income Statement measures the success of a company's operations; it provides investors and creditors with information needed to determine the enterprise's profitability and creditworthiness. A company has earned net income when its total revenues exceed its total expenses. A company has a net loss when total expenses exceed total revenues.

The Statement of Retained Earnings

Retained earnings is the amount of profit a company invests in itself (i.e., profit that is not used to pay back debt or distributed to shareholders as a dividend). The Statement of Retained Earnings is a reconciliation of the Retained Earnings account from the beginning to the end of the year. When a company announces income or declares dividends, this information is reflected in the Statement of Retained Earnings. Net income increases the Retained Earnings account. Net losses and dividend payments decrease Retained Earnings.

Here is an example of a basic Statement of Retained Earnings:

Media Entertainment, Inc
Statement of Retained Earnings
(For the year ended December 31, 2005)

Retained Earnings, January 1, 2005	$200,000
Plus: Net income for the year	43,000
	243,000
Less: Dividends declared	(12,000)
Retained Earnings, December 31, 2005	$ 231,000

As you can probably tell by looking at this example, the Statement of Retained Earnings doesn't provide any new information not already reflected in other financial statements. But it does provide additional information about what management is doing with the company's earnings. Management may be reinvesting the company's net income into the business by retaining part or all of its earnings, distributing its current income to shareholders, or distributing current and accumulated income to shareholders. (Investors can use this information to align their investment strategy with the strategy of a company's management. An investor interested in growth and returns on capital may be more inclined to invest in a company that reinvests its resources into the company for the purpose of generating additional resources. Conversely, an investor interested in receiving current income is more inclined to invest in a company that pays quarterly dividend distributions to shareholders.)

The Statement of Cash Flows

Remember that the Income Statement provides information about the economic resources involved in the operation of a company. However, the Income Statement does not provide information about the actual source and use of cash generated during its operations. That's because obtaining and using economic resources doesn't always involve cash. For example, let's say you went shopping and bought a new mountain bike on your credit card in July – but didn't pay the bill until August. Although the store did not receive cash in July, the sale would still be considered July revenue. The

Statement of Cash Flows presents a detailed summary of all of the cash inflows and outflows during the period and is divided into three sections based on three types of activity:

- **Cash flows from operating activities:** Includes the cash effects of transactions involved in calculating net income.

- **Cash flows from investing activities**: Basically, cash from non-operating activities or activities outside the normal scope of business. This involves items classified as assets in the Balance Sheet and includes the purchase and sale of equipment and investments.

- **Cash flows from financing activities:** Involves items classified as liabilities and equity in the Balance Sheet; it includes the payment of dividends as well as issuing payment of debt or equity.

This example shows the basic format of the Statement of Cash Flows:

Media Entertainment, Inc
Statement of Cash Flows
(For the year ended December 31, 2005)

Cash flows provided from operating activities		
Net Income		33,000
Depreciation Expense		10,000
Increase in Accounts Receivable	(26,000)	
Increase in Accounts Payable	7,000	(19,000)
Net cash provided by operating activities		24,000
Cash flows provided from investing activities		
Purchase of Building	(19,000)	
Sale of Long-Term Investment	35,000	
Net cash provided by investing activities		16,000
Cash flows provided from financing activities		
Payment of Dividends	(12,000)	
Issuance of Common Stock	10,000	
Net cash provided by financing activities		(2,000)
Net increase (decrease) in cash		38,000
Cash at the beginning of the year		165,000
Cash at the end of the year		203,000

As you can tell be looking at the above example, the Statement of Cash Flows gets its information from all three of the other financial statements:

- Net income from the Income Statement is shown in the section "cash flows from operating activities."

- Dividends from the Statement of Retained Earnings is shown in the section "cash flows from financing activities."

- Investments, Accounts Payable, and other asset and liability accounts from the Balance Sheet are shown in all three sections.

Market Valuation

Now let's look at the major techniques of valuation. We'll begin with market valuation, as it is the simplest way to value a publicly traded firm. A publicly traded firm is one that is registered on a stock exchange (like the New York Stock Exchange or Nasdaq). The company's stock can be bought and sold on that exchange. Most companies we are familiar with, such as The Coca-Cola Company, IBM, and General Motors, are publicly traded. Every publicly traded company is required to publish an annual report, which includes financial figures such as annual revenues, income, and expenses. The 10Ks (Annual Financials) and 10Qs (Quarterly Financials) for publicly traded firms are available online through the SEC Edgar database, www.edgar-online.com.

The value of a publicly traded firm is easy to calculate. All you need to do is find the company's stock price (the price of a single share), multiply it by the number of shares outstanding, and you have the equity market value of the company. (This is also known as market capitalization or "market cap"). The market price of a single share of stock is readily available from publications like *The Wall Street Journal* and from various quote services available on the Internet; the number of shares outstanding can be obtained from the cover of the most recent 10-K or 10-Q of the company, or from web sites such as Yahoo! Finance, Hoover's Online, and cnnfn.com.

Visit the Vault Finance Career Channel at **www.vault.com/finance** — with
insider firm profiles, message boards, the Vault Finance Job Board and more.

VAULT CAREER LIBRARY

27

Example:

Company A stock price	$60/share
No. of shares outstanding	200 million
Equity Market Value (market cap) =	$60 x 200 million = $12 billion

Once you determine the market value of a firm, you need to figure out either the discount or premium that it would sell for if the company were put on the market. When a company sells for a discount it is selling for a value lower than the market value; when it sells for a premium, it is selling for a value greater than the market value. Whether a company sells at a premium or a discount depends on those supply and demand forces you learned about in Econ 101. Typically, if someone wants to acquire a firm, it will sell for a price above the market value of the firm. This is referred to as an acquisition premium. If the acquisition is a hostile takeover, or if there is an auction, the premiums are pushed even higher. The premiums are generally decided by the perception of the synergies resulting from the purchase or merger. (See chapter on M&A.)

Discounted Cash Flow (DCF)

The DCF analysis is the most thorough way to value a company, and second-year MBAs should expect to be tested on their ability to do a DCF in a finance interview. There are two ways to value a company using the DCF approach:

- Adjusted Present Value (APV) method
- Weighted Average Cost of Capital (WACC) method

Both methods require calculation of a company's free cash flows (FCF) as well as the net present value (NPV) of these FCFs. Before we look at these methods, we'll examine a few underlying concepts: net present value, the Capital Asset Pricing Model (CAPM), free cash flows, and terminal year value.

Net Present Value

What do we mean when we talk about net present value? We'll explain this important concept with a simple example. Let's say you had an arrangement under which you were set to receive $20 from a friend one year from now. Now let's say for some reason that you decide you don't want to wait for a year and would rather have the money today. How much should you be willing to accept today? More than $20, $20, or less than $20?

In general, a dollar today is worth more than a dollar tomorrow for two simple reasons. First, a dollar today can be invested at a risk-free interest rate (think savings account or U.S. government bonds), and can earn a return. A dollar tomorrow is worth less because it has missed out on the interest you would have earned on that dollar had you invested it today. Second, inflation diminishes the buying power of future money.

A discount rate is the rate you choose to discount the future value of your money. A discount rate can be understood as the expected return from a project that matches the risk profile of the project in which you'd invest your $20.

Note: The discount rate is different than the opportunity cost of the money. Opportunity cost is a measure of the opportunity lost. Discount rate is a measure of the risk. These are two separate concepts.

To express the relationship between the present value and future value, we use the following formula:

$$\text{Present Value} = \frac{\text{Future Value}}{(1 + r_d)^n}$$

Here, "r_d" is the discount rate, and "n" is the number of years in the future.

The method of calculating the discount rate is different depending on the method of valuation used (i.e., APV method vs. WACC method). Although the discount rate varies, the concept of NPV, or net present value, is the same.

Let's say a series of cash flows is expressed as the following:

Year	1	2	3	4	5	6	7	8
Free Cash Flows	FCF_1	FCF_2	FCF_3	FCF_4	FCF_5	FCF_6	FCF_7	FCF_8

Visit the Vault Finance Career Channel at **www.vault.com/finance** — with
insider firm profiles, message boards, the Vault Finance Job Board and more.

VAULT CAREER LIBRARY

29

Net present value (NPV) in Year 0 of future cash flows is calculated with the following formula:

$$NPV = \frac{FCF_1}{(1 + r_d)^1} + \frac{FCF_2}{(1 + r_d)^2} + \frac{FCF_3}{(1 + r_d)^3} + ... + \frac{FCF_8}{(1 + r_d)^8}$$

or

$$NPV = \sum_{i=1}^{n} \left(\frac{FCF_i}{(1 + r_d)^i} \right)$$

Here again, r_d is the discount rate, which is calculated differently depending on whether you use APV or WACC (to be explained later).

Capital Asset Pricing Model (CAPM)

In order to find the appropriate discount rate used to discount the company's cash flows, you use the Capital Asset Pricing Model, or (CAPM). This is a model used to calculate the expected return on your investment, also referred to as expected return on equity. It is a linear model with one independent variable, Beta. Beta represents relative volatility of the given investment with respect to the market. For example, if the Beta of an investment is 1, the returns on the investment (stock/bond/portfolio) vary identically with the market returns. A Beta less than 1, like 0.5, means the investment is less volatile than the market. So if the Dow Jones Industrial Average goes up or down 20 percent the next day, a less volatile stock (i.e., Beta < 1) would be expected to go up or down 10 percent. A Beta of greater than 1, like 1.5, means the investment is more volatile than the market. A company in a volatile industry (think Internet company) would be expected to have a Beta greater than 1. A company whose value does not vary much, like an electric utility, would be expected to have a Beta under 1.

Mathematically, CAPM is calculated as

$$r_e = r_f + \beta (r_m - r_f)$$

Here:

r_e = Discount rate for an all-equity firm

r_f = Risk-free rate (The Treasury bill rate for the period over which the cash projections are being considered. For example, if we are considering a 10-year period, then the risk-free rate is the rate for the 10-year U.S. Treasury note.)

r_m = Market return

$r_m - r_f$ = Excess market return (This is the excess annual return of the stock market over a U.S. Treasury bond over a long period of time. This is usually assumed to be 7 percent for the U.S. Market.)

β = Equity Beta

Equity Beta is given in various sources like Value Line or Internet sites like Yahoo! Finance. If the firm you are valuing is not publicly traded, then you need to find a firm with a similar Balance Sheet and Income Statement that is publicly traded. (When calculating CAPM you should be careful to use the "equity Beta" value, and not "assets Beta.") If you have information for Beta assets rather than Beta equity, you can derive Beta equity using the following relationship:

$$\beta_A = (\beta_E)\frac{(E)}{(D+E)} + (1 - t)\frac{(D)}{(D+E)}(\beta_D)$$

Here:

D =   Market value of debt (usually the book value of debt)

E =   Market value of equity (the number of shares outstanding x share price) (Also known as "market cap.")

β_D =   Beta debt (usually one can assume this to be equal to 0)

t =   Corporate taxes, (usually assumed to be 35%)

Therefore:

$$\beta_E \;=\; \beta_A \frac{(D + E)}{(E)}$$

Free cash flows

To capture the characteristics of an all-equity firm we recalculate a company's cash flows as if the firm had no debt. The free cash flow (FCF) of an all-equity firm in year (i) can be calculated as:

FCF_i = Earnings Before Interest and Taxes x (1 - t)

+ Depreciation & Amortization

- Capital Expenditure ("CapEx")

- Net increase in working capital (or + net *decrease* in working capital)

+ Other relevant cash flows for an all equity firm

Here:

Earnings Before Interest and Taxes (or EBIT) can be obtained from the Income Statement (see section on major accounting concepts).

t = Corporate tax rate, usually assumed to be 35%.

Depreciation & Amortization of a firm can be obtained from the firm's Balance Sheet (see section on major accounting concepts).

Capital Expenditure and Net increase in working capital can be obtained from the Statement of Cash Flows.

Other relevant cash flows for an all-equity firm would be items like asset sale proceeds (selling a major piece of real estate, for example) or the use of tax loss carry-forwards or tax credits.

While all of these items can be found in the firm's financial statements for historical periods, the free cash flow used for DCF analysis is expected future free cash flow. Bankers will typically construct projections, using a combination of guidelines from the company and a derivation of reasonable estimates using their own assumptions. While historical financial statements are helpful in constructing projections, DCF analysis can only be done with future cash flow projections.

Terminal year calculation

The terminal year represents the year (usually 10 years in the future) when the growth of the company is considered stabilized.

In other words...

The cash flows of the first 10 years are determined by company management or a financial analyst, based on predictions and forecasts of what will happen. Then, a terminal year value needs to be calculated assuming that after year 10 the cash flows of the company keep growing at a constant "g." Values of "g" are typically not as high as the first 10 years of growth, which are considered unstabilized growth periods. Instead, "g" represents the amount the company can feasibly grow forever once it has stabilized (after 10 years).

The value of the terminal year cash flows (that is, the value in year 10) is given by:

$$\text{TY FCF} = \frac{FCF_{10}\,(1 + g)}{(r_d - g)}$$

The present value of the terminal year cash flows (that is, the value today) is given by:

$$\text{PV (TY FCF)} = \frac{\text{TY FCF}}{(1 + r_d)^{10}}$$

or

$$\text{PV (TY FCF)} = \frac{FCF_{10}\,(1 + g)}{(1 + r_d)^{10}\,(r_d - g)}$$

Adding it up

Adding the discounted value of the first 10 year FCFs, and the terminal year FCFs (CFs after year 10 into perpetuity) gives us the value of the company under the DCF analysis.

Calculating discount rates

Remember when we said that there are several ways of calculating discount rates? We'll now look at the two most popular methods of discounted cash flow (DCF) analysis tested in finance interviews: the WACC (Weighted Average Cost of Capital) and APV (Adjusted Present Value). The key difference between the two methods is the way in which the discount rate is calculated. For WACC, we calculate the discount rate for leveraged equity (reL) using the capital asset pricing model (CAPM); for APV, we calculate the discount rate for an all-equity firm (reU).

WACC

For WACC, the discount rate is calculated with the following formula:

$$r_{dWACC} = \frac{(E)}{(D + E)} (r_e^L) + \frac{(D)}{(D + E)} (1 - t)(r_D)$$

Here:

D   = Market value of debt
E   = Market value of equity
r_D = Discount rate for debt = Average interest rate on long-term debt
r_e^L = Discount rate for (leveraged) equity (calculated using the CAPM)

Note: The terms (E)/(D + E) and (D)/(D + E) represent the "target" equity and debt ratios (also referred to as the equity-to-debt and debt-to-equity ratios).

CAPM:

$$r_e^L = r_f + \beta^L (r_m - r_f)$$

Here:

r_f = Risk-free rate = the Treasury bond rate for the period for which the projections are being considered
r_m = Market return
$r_m - r_f$ = Excess market return
β^L = Leveraged Beta

The value of leveraged Beta can be derived from the unleveraged Beta using the equation below, in a process also referred to as "unlevering the Beta":

$$\beta^L = \beta^U \left[1 + (1 - t) \frac{(D)}{(E)} \right]$$

Here:

β^U = Unleveraged Beta (Again, β^U for a specific company can be obtained from Value Line or online sources like Yahoo!)

APV

For the APV calculation the discount rate is calculated with the following formula:

$$r_e^U = r_f + \beta^U (r_m - r_f)$$

Here:

β^U = Unleveraged Beta

Thus we see the key difference between WACC and APV. With the APV calculation, we take the unleveraged equity discount rate (the discount rate that assumes that a company has no debt), rather than a leveraged (historical) discount rate that the WACC calculation uses.

To summarize:

Method	Discount Rate	Type of Firm (Assumption)	Beta
APV	r_e^U	all equity	β^U
WACC	r_e^L	leveraged/historical	β^L

So suppose a company has debt. Obviously, the APV does not capture the real value of a comapny in this case. Why? Because interest payments are tax deductible. Hence, to find the value of a company using APV, we add in the value of the debt tax shield, or the amount of money a company saves by not having to pay interest on debt. To compensate for this difference we add a value for the debt tax shield separately to arrive at an overall valuation of the company. The debt tax shield (DTS) for any year is given by:

$$\text{DTS} = (t)(r_D)(D)$$

Here:

D = Total debt for the company that year

r_D = Weighted average interest rate on that debt calculated for each year of the projected cash flows

t   = Corporate tax rate

This principle is the main reason for the emergence of the LBO (leveraged buyout) shops, including Kohlberg Kravis Roberts & Co. (KKR) and its famous takeover of RJR Nabisco, which inspired the bestseller *Barbarians at the Gate*. KKR borrowed money (issued debt) to buy RJR Nabisco at a price well above the market price. Since the company had no debt before the takeover and has historically had highly reliable cash flows, KKR was able to increase the company's value through a financial restructuring and save on taxes through the use of interest payments on debt and its accompanying write-offs.

The tricky question now is: What discount rate should be used for calculating the present value of the DTS? The answer is the discount rate that would best capture the risk associated with the DTS. If you assume that the ability to use the tax shield is as risky as the cash flows to an all-equity firm, we would use the reU. If you assume that the tax shield is as risky as the ability to repay the debt, then the discount rate should be the average interest rate, or rD.

Note: The debt tax shield is similarly calculated for the terminal year and discounted to the present year.

APV with DTS = APV without DTS + DTS

One simple approximation for DTS that can be used for most back-of-the-envelope calculations in an interview is:

DTS = APV without DTS X (Tax rate (t) X Long-term debt rate (L))

Here:

t   = Tax rate
L   = Leverage ratio (also referred to as the long-term debt ratio) = $D/(D + E)$

The main difference between the WACC and APV methods is that the WACC takes the "target" debt-to-equity ratio to calculate the discount rate. However, a target debt-to-equity ratio is not reached until a few years in the future. Hence the method is not "academically complete." The APV method takes this into consideration and looks at an "all-equity" firm.

However, the difference that amounts from assuming a target debt-to-equity ratio is very small; most investment banks use the WACC method even though most business schools teach both methods. The difference between the two methods will become clearer as we go through an example of how to calculate the appropriate discount rate.

Step 1: Assumptions

You are given the following information for the company you are valuing:

	Year 1	Year 2	Year 3	Year 4
EBIT	7.0	7.5	7.9	8.4
Depreciation	2.9	2.7	2.7	2.6
Capital Expenditures	1.5	2.5	2.5	3.0
Increase in Working Capital	0.8	1.5	1.5	0.9

Tax Rate (t)	35%
Book Value Debt (D)	7.0
Book Value Equity (E_{book})	10.0
Market Value Equity (E_{market})	15.0
Beta (historical) (β_L)	1.5
Long-term T-Bond rate (r_f)	10.0%
Long-term debt rate (r_D)	12.0%
Long-term growth rate (g)	6.0%
Long-term risk premium ($r_m - r_f$)	8.0%

Step 2: Cash flows

Free cash flow to all equity firm = EBIT (1 - t) + Depr. - CAPX - Ch NWC.

Plugging in our data, we get:

Year One   =   7.0 (1 - 0.35) + 2.9 - 1.5 - 0.8 = 5.15
Year Two   =   7.5 (1 - 0.35) + 2.7 - 2.5 - 1.5 = 3.58
Year Three =   7.9 (1 - 0.35) + 2.7 - 2.5 - 1.5 = 3.84
Year Four   =   8.4 (1 - 0.35) + 2.6 - 3.0 - 0.9 = 4.16

So our free cash flows look like this:

	Year 1	Year 2	Year 3	Year 4
FCF	5.15	3.58	3.84	4.16

Step 3: Discount rates

APV

Remember that there are two ways to determine a discount rate. Let's begin with the APV analysis

---

First get ß^U from the ß^L of 1.50

$$\beta^U = \frac{\beta^L}{\left[1 + (1 - t)\dfrac{(D)}{E_{(market\ value)}}\right]}$$

$$\beta^U = \frac{1.50}{1 + (1 - 0.35)\dfrac{(7.0)}{(15.0)}} = 1.15$$

$$r_e^U = r_f + \beta^U (r_m - r_f)$$

$$r_e^U = 0.10 + (1.15)(0.08) = \mathbf{0.0192\ or\ 19.2\%}$$

Hence, the expected return on equity for an all-equity firm would be 19.2 percent. We will use this as the discount rate for the APV analysis.

Remember:

ß^L = Beta for a firm with debt, or historical Beta (leveraged/historical Beta)

ß^U = Beta for the equivalent firm without debt, or an all-equity firm (unleveraged Beta)

WACC

Let's now look at the WACC method. For WACC, we need to know what the target (long-term) debt-to-capital ratio for this company is. Let's assume that it is 40 percent. That is, in the long run, this company expects to finance its projects with 40 percent debt and 60 percent equity.

First, we need to calculate ß^L

$$\beta^L = \beta^U \left[1 + (1 - t) \frac{(D)}{(E)} \right]$$

$$\beta^L = 1.15 \left[1 + (1 - 0.35) \frac{(0.4)}{(0.6)} \right]$$

$$= 1.64$$

$$r_e^L = r_f + \beta^L (r_m - r_f)$$

$$r_e^L = (0.10) + (1.64)(0.08) = \mathbf{0.2312 \ or \ 23.12\%}$$

Note: Here we calculate our expected return on equity, or reL, using the target debt-to-equity ratio. We use this r_e^L for all years whether or not that target ratio has been matched or not. Since our long-term debt rate is 12.0 percent, and our long-term debt is 40 percent, we can now calculate WACC.

$$r_{WACC} = \frac{(E)}{(D+E)} (r_e^L) + \frac{(D)}{(D+E)} (1 - t)(r_D)$$

$$= 0.6 \times 0.2312 + 0.4 \times (1 - 0.35) \times 0.13$$

$$= \mathbf{0.1699 \ or \ 17.0\%}$$

Step 4: Terminal value

We assume that the company operates forever. But, we only have four years of cash flow. We need to put a value on all the cash flows after Year Four. The Year Four cash flow is 4.16 and we expect it to grow at 5 percent a year. The value of all cash flows after Year Four (as of the end of Year Four) can be calculated with our Terminal Value formula.

Using APV

$$\text{TY FCF} = \frac{FCF_4 (1 + g)}{(r_d - g)}$$

$$\text{TY FCF} = \frac{4.16 \times (1 + 0.05)}{(0.192 - 0.05)} = \mathbf{30.76}$$

Using WACC

$$\text{TY FCF} = \frac{FCF_4 (1 + g)}{(r_d - g)}$$

$$\text{TY FCF} = \frac{4.16 \times (1 + 0.05)}{(0.173 - 0.05)} = \mathbf{35.51}$$

Step 5: Taking the NPV of all the cash flows

Now we have to add up our cash flows

APV

	Year 1	Year 2	Year 3	Year 4
FCF	5.15	3.58	3.84	4.16

Add terminal value = 30.76

FCF$_{adjusted}$	5.15	3.58	3.84	34.92

Using these cash flows, and our discount rate of 19.2 percent, we can calculate the net present value.

$$NPV = \frac{FCF_1}{(1 + r_d)^1} + \frac{FCF_2}{(1 + r_d)^2} + \frac{FCF_3}{(1 + r_d)^3} + \frac{FCF_4}{(1 + r_d)^4}$$

$$NPV = \frac{5.15}{(1 + 0.192)} + \frac{3.58}{(1 + 0.192)^2} + \frac{3.84}{(1 + 0.192)^3} + \frac{34.92}{(1 + 0.192)^4}$$

$$NPV = 4.32 + 2.52 + 2.27 + 17.30 = \mathbf{26.41} \text{ (approximately)}$$

Visit the Vault Finance Career Channel at **www.vault.com/finance** — with insider firm profiles, message boards, the Vault Finance Job Board and more.

V/\ULT CAREER LIBRARY

41

Let's add up the cash flows for the WACC method:

WACC

	Year 1	Year 2	Year 3	Year 4
FCF	5.15	3.58	3.84	4.16

Add terminal value = 35.51

FCF$_{adjusted}$	5.15	3.58	3.84	39.67

Using these cash flows, with a discount rate of 17.0 percent, we can calculate an NPV ($r = r_{WACC}$)

$$NPV = \frac{FCF_1}{(1+r)^1} + \frac{FCF_2}{(1+r)^2} + \frac{FCF_3}{(1+r)^3} + \frac{FCF_4}{(1+r)^4}$$

$$NPV = \frac{5.15}{(1+0.17)} + \frac{3.58}{(1+0.17)^2} + \frac{3.84}{(1+0.17)^3} + \frac{34.92}{(1+0.17)^4}$$

$$NPV = 4.4 + 2.6 + 2.4 + 18.6 = \mathbf{28.0} \text{ (approximately)}$$

Step 6: Figuring out the company's value

For WACC, we are done with our calculation – the value of the company is approximately $28.0.

For APV, however, we add the present value of the interest tax shields (DTS). We use the following formula:

To summarize:

	APV	WACC
Discounted value of FCF	$26.41	$28.0
Value of tax shield	$3.7	
Total	$30.1	$28.0

The APV and WACC methods make slightly different assumptions about the value of interest tax shields, resulting in slightly different values.

Visit the Vault Finance Career Channel at **www.vault.com/finance** — with
insider firm profiles, message boards, the Vault Finance Job Board and more.

VAULT CAREER LIBRARY 43

Comparable Transactions

To use the "comparable transactions" technique of valuing a company, you need to look at the "comparable" transactions that have taken place in the industry and accompanying relevant metrics such as "multiples" or ratios (e.g., price paid: EBITDA). For example, when NationsBank was considering acquiring Montgomery Securities, it likely studied comparable transactions, such as Bankers Trust's acquisition of Alex Brown or Bank of America's acquisition of Robertson Stephens. In other words, NationsBank looked at other acquisitions of investment banks by financial institutions that had taken place in the recent past, ascertained the relevant multiples at which these firms were acquired (EBIT or Book Value, for example) and applied these multiples to the company which they were trying to value.

With the comparable transactions method, you are looking for a key valuation parameter. That is, were the companies in those transactions valued as a multiple of EBIT, EBITDA, revenue, or some other parameter? If you figure out what the key valuation parameter is, you can examine at what multiples of those parameters the comparable companies were valued. You can then use a similar approach to value the company being considered.

As an example, let's assume that there is an Internet start-up called echicago.com that is planning to go public. Let's also say that this is a health care Internet company. The question the company's financial management, their investment bankers, and the portfolio managers who are planning to buy stock in the company will ask is: "How much is the company worth?" To obtain a value for the company, they can look at recent comparable transactions. For example, suppose eharvard.com and estanford.com are other health care Internet companies that have recently successfully gone public. The financials of the companies are summarized below (assume all companies have no net debt, so their Equity and Enterprise Values are identical):

Company	Value (Market Cap) [mil]	Sales [mil]	EBITDA [mil]	Earnings (Losses) [mil]	Sales Multiples (Market Cap/Sales)
echicago.com	?	80	20	(10)	?
estanford.com	2100	70	17	(12)	30
eharvard.com	3000	75	18	(8)	40

Because the three companies are in the same industry and have similar financials, the transaction for echicago.com can be valued at multiples similar to those used for the other two. The value for echicago.com could be anywhere from 30 x 80 to 40 x 80, i.e., 2,400 to 3,200 millions of dollars, or $2.4 billion to $3.2 billion. (Bankers would value the company using this range in valuation; at the time of heavy speculation in Internet stocks, however, we would not be surprised if investors valued the company at an even higher price.)

Multiple Analysis or Comparable Company Analysis

Quite often, there is not enough information to determine the valuation using the comparable transactions method. In these cases, you can value a company based on market valuation multiples, which you can do using more readily available information. Examples of these valuation multiples include price/earning multiples (also known as P/E ratios, this method, which compares a company's market capitalization to its annual income, is the most commonly used multiple) EBITDA multiples, and others. Once you have done this, you can add debt to ascertain enterprise value. When using these methods, you look at which multiples are used for other companies in the industry to ascertain equity value.

Let's look at an example. What is the value of a company in the semiconductor industry with $100 million in net debt that posts annual sales of $180 million, EBITDA of $70 million, and earnings of $40 million (let's call it Wharton Semiconductor). Companies in the semiconductor industry might be valued with sales, EBITDA or earning multiples. The numbers used for EBITDA or earnings might be figured for the 12 months trailing (the previous 12 months), the last fiscal year, 12 months projected, or the next fiscal year projected. These figures can be obtained from research reports published by various research departments within investment banks or brokerage houses.

Let's assume that there are four semiconductor companies similar to Wharton Semiconductor. An investment bank would perform a "Common Stock Comparison" to determine relevant multiples:

Company	Value (Market Cap)	Sales	EBITDA	Earnings
Chicago Semiconductor	900	220	115	82
Harvard Semiconductor	700	190	90	60
Kellogg Semiconductor	650	280	68	42
Stanford Semiconductor	320	150	45	26

Company	Sales Multiples $\left(\frac{\text{Market Cap}}{\text{Sales}}\right)$	EBITDA Multiples $\left(\frac{\text{Market Cap}}{\text{EBITDA}}\right)$	Price-to-Earnings Multiples $\left(\frac{\text{Market Cap}}{\text{Earnings}}\right)$
Chicago Semiconductor	4.1	7.8	11.0
Harvard Semiconductor	3.7	7.8	11.7
Kellogg Semiconductor	2.3	9.6	15.5
Stanford Semiconductor	2.1	7.1	12.3
AVERAGE	**3.1**	**8.1**	**12.6**

Notice above that Enterprise Value is divided by sales or EBITDA to ascertain the sales and EBITDA multiples, while Equity Value is divided by Net Income to ascertain the price-to-earnings multiple.

Using the average multiples from the Common Stock Comparison, we can estimate Wharton Semiconductor's value as follows:

Using the sales multiple: Wharton's sales of $180 million x 3.1 (average sales multiple) = $558 million (Enterprise Value) - $100 million (Net Debt) = $458 million (Equity Value)

Using the EBITDA multiple: Wharton's EBITDA of $70 million x 8.1 (average EBITDA multiple) = $565 million (Enterprise Value) - $100 million (Net Debt) = $465 million (Equity Value)

Using the price-to-earnings multiple: Wharton's earnings of $40 million x 12.6 (average price-to-earnings multiple) = $505 million (Equity Value)

So using the multiples method, we can estimate the Equity Value of Wharton Semiconductor at between $449 and $505 million. This means that, adding in debt, we arrive at Wharton's Enterprise Value of between $549 and $605 million.

Questions

1. What is the difference between the Income Statement and the Statement of Cash Flows?

The Income Statement is a record of Revenues and Expenses while the Statement of Cash Flows records the actual cash that has either come into or left the company. The Statement of Cash Flows has the following categories: Operating Cash Flows, Investing Cash Flows, and Financing Cash Flows.

Interestingly, a company can be profitable as shown in the Income Statement, but still go bankrupt if it doesn't have the cash flow to meet interest payments.

2. What is the link between the Balance Sheet and the Income Statement?

The main link between the two statements is that profits generated in the Income Statement get added to shareholder's equity on the Balance Sheet as Retained Earnings. Also, debt on the Balance Sheet is used to calculate interest expense in the Income Statement.

Visit the Vault Finance Career Channel at **www.vault.com/finance** — with insider firm profiles, message boards, the Vault Finance Job Board and more.

VAULT CAREER LIBRARY   47

3. What is the link between the Balance Sheet and the Statement of Cash Flows?

The Statement of Cash Flows starts with the beginning cash balance, which comes from the Balance Sheet. Also, Cash from Operations is derived using the changes in Balance Sheet accounts (such as Accounts Payable, Accounts Receivable, etc.). The net increase in cash flow for the prior year goes back onto the next year's Balance Sheet .

4. What is EBITDA?

A proxy for cash flow, EBITDA is Earnings Before Interest, Taxes, Depreciation, and Amortization.

5. Say you knew a company's net income. How would you figure out its "free cash flow"?

Start with the company's Net Income. Then add back Depreciation and Amortization. Subtract the company's Capital Expenditures (called "CapEx" for short, this is how much money the company invests each year in plant and equipment). The number you get is the company's free cash flow:

Net Income

\+ Depreciation and Amortization

\- Capital Expenditures

\- Increase (or + decrease) in net working capital

\= Free Cash Flow (FCF)

6. Walk me through the major line items on a Cash Flow statement.

The answer: first the Beginning Cash Balance, then Cash from Operations, then Cash from Investing Activities, then Cash from Financing Activities, and finally the Ending Cash Balance.

7. What happens to each of the three primary financial statements when you change a) gross margin b) capital expenditures c) any other change?

Think about the definitions of the variables that change. For example, gross margin is gross profit/sales, or the extent to which sales of sold inventory exceeds costs. Hence, if a) gross margin were to decrease, then gross profit decreases relative to sales. Thus, for the Income Statement, you would probably pay lower taxes, but if nothing else changed, you would likely have lower net income. The cash flow statement would be affected in the top line with less cash likely coming in. Hence, if everything else remained the same, you would likely have less cash. Going to the Balance Sheet, you would not only have less cash, but to balance that effect, you would have lower shareholder's equity.

b) If capital expenditure were to say, decrease, then first, the level of capital expenditures would decrease on the Statement of Cash Flows. This would increase the level of cash on the balance sheet, but decrease the level of property, plant and equipment, so total assets stay the same. On the income statement, the depreciation expense would be lower in subsequent years, so net income would be higher, which would increase cash and shareholder's equity in the future.

c) Just be sure you understand the interplay between the three sheets. Remember that changing one sheet has ramifications on all the other statements both today and in the future.

8. How do you value a company?

Valuing a company is one of the most popular technical tasks you will be asked to perform in finance interviews. Remember the several methods that we discussed, and good luck. MBAs looking for I-banking or finance in a company positions are sure to get this question.

One basic answer to this question is to discount the company's projected cash flows using a "risk-adjusted discount rate." This process involves several steps. First you must project a company's cash flows for 10 years. Then you must choose a constant growth rate after 10 years going forward. Finally, you must choose an appropriate discount rate. After projecting the first five or 10 years performance, you add in a "Terminal Value," which represents the present value of all the future cash flows another 10 years. You can calculate the Terminal Value in one of two ways: (1) you take the earnings of the last year you projected, say year 10, and multiply it by some market multiple like 20 times earnings, use that as your terminal value; or (2) you take the last year, say year 10, and assume some constant growth rate after that like 10 percent. The present value of this growing stream of payments after year 10 is the Terminal Value. Finally, to figure out what "discount rate" you would use to discount the company's cash flows, tell your interviewer you would use the "Capital Asset Pricing Model" (or

Visit the Vault Finance Career Channel at **www.vault.com/finance** — with insider firm profiles, message boards, the Vault Finance Job Board and more.

VAULT CAREER LIBRARY   **49**

"CAPM"). (In a nutshell, CAPM says that the proper discount rate to use is the risk-free interest rate adjusted upwards to reflect this particular company's market risk or "Beta.") For a more advanced answer, discuss the APV and WACC methods.

You should also mention other methods of valuing a company, including looking at "comparables" – that is, how other similar companies were valued recently as a multiple of their sales, net income, or some other measure.

9. The CEO of a $500 million company has called you, her investment banker. She wants to sell the company. She wants to know how much she can expect for the company today.

It might sound different, but this is the same question as No. 8: How do you value a company?

10. What is the formula for the Capital Asset Pricing Model?

The Capital Asset Pricing Model is used to calculate the expected return on an investment. Beta for a company is a measure of the relative volatility of the given investment with respect to the market, i.e., if Beta is 1, the returns on the investment (stock/bond/portfolio) vary identically with the market's returns. Here "the market" refers to a well diversified index such as the S&P 500. The formula for CAPM is as follows:

$$\textbf{CAPM:}$$
$$r_e{}^L = r_f + \beta^L (r_m - r_f)$$

Here:

r_f = Risk-free rate = the Treasury bond rate for the period for which the projections are being considered

r_m = Market return

$r_m - r_f$ = Excess market return

β^L = Leveraged Beta

$r_e{}^L$ = Discount rate for (leveraged) equity (calculated using the CAPM)

11. Why might there be multiple valuations for a single company?

As this chapter has discussed, there are several different methods by which one can value a company. And even if you use the rigorously academic DCF analysis, the two main methods (the WACC and APV method) make different assumptions about interest tax shields, which can lead to different valuations.

12. How do you calculate the terminal value of a company?

Terminal year value is calculated by taking a given year in the future at which a company is stable (usually year 10), assuming perpetually stable growth after that year, using a perpetuity formula to come up with the value in that year based on future cash flows, and discounting that value back to the present day. This method uses the following formula.

$$\text{TY FCF} = \frac{\text{FCF}_{10}\,(1 + g)}{(r_d - g)}$$

Here "g" is an assumed growth rate and rd is the discount rate. Remember that you could also calculate the terminal value of a company by taking a multiple of terminal year cash flows, and discounting that back to the present to arrive at an answer. This alternative method might be used in some instances because it is less dependent on the assumed growth rate (g).

13. Why are the P/E multiples for a company in London different than that of the same company in the States?

The P/E multiples can be different in the two countries even if all other factors are constant because of the difference in the way earnings are recorded. Overall market valuations in American markets tend to be higher than those in the U.K.

14. What are the different multiples that can be used to value a company?

The most commonly used multiple is price-to-earnings multiple, or "P/E ratio." Other multiples that are used include revenue, EBITDA, EBIT, and book value. The relevant multiple depends on the industry. For example, Internet companies are often valued with revenue multiples; this explains why companies with low profits can have such high market caps. Companies in the metals and mining industry are valued using EBITDA.

As discussed in the section on valuation, not only should you be aware of the financial metric being used, you should know the time period the metric used represents: for example, earnings in a P/E ratio can be for the previous or projected 12 months, or for the previous or projected fiscal year.

15. How do you get the discount rate for an all-equity firm?

You use the Capital Asset Pricing Model, or CAPM.

16. Can I apply CAPM in Latin American markets?

CAPM was developed for use in the U.S. markets, however, it is presently the best known tool for calculating discount rates. Hence, while CAPM is not exact, it is a good framework for thinking about and analyzing discount rates outside of the U.S. as fundamentally, markets are based on similar principles.

17. How much would you pay for a company with $50 million in revenue and $5 million in profit?

If this is all the information you are given you can use the comparable transaction or multiples method to value this company (rather than the DCF method). To use the multiples method, you can examine common stock information of comparable companies in the same industry, to get average industry multiples of price-to-earnings. You can then apply that multiple to find the given company's value.

18. What is the difference between the APV and WACC?

WACC incorporates the effect of tax shields into the discount rate used to calculate the present value of cash flows. WACC is typically calculated using actual data and numbers from balance sheets for companies or industries.

APV adds the present value of the financing effects (most commonly, the debt tax shield) to the net present value assuming an all-equity value, and calculates the adjusted present value. The APV approach is particularly useful in cases where subsidized costs of financing are more complex, such as in a leveraged buyout.

19. How would you value a company with no revenue?

First you would make reasonable assumptions about the company's projected revenues (and projected cash flows) for future years. Then you would calculate the Net Present Value of these cash flows.

20. What is Beta?

Beta is the value that represents a stock's volatility with respect to overall market volatility.

21. How do you unlever a company's Beta?

Unlevering a company's Beta means calculating the Beta under the assumption that it is an all-equity firm. The formula is as follows:

$$\beta^L = \beta^U \left[1 + (1 - t)\frac{(D)}{(E)} \right]$$

22. Name three companies that are undervalued and tell me why you think they are undervalued.

This is a very popular question for equity research and portfolio management jobs. Here you have to do your homework. Study the stocks you like and value them using various methods: DCF, multiples, comparable transactions, etc. Then choose several undervalued (and overvalued) stocks, and be prepared to back up your assessment, using financial and strategy information.

For example, let's say that Coke received some bad PR recently and its stock took a hammering in the market. However, the earnings of Coke are not expected to decrease significantly because of the negative publicity (or at least that's your analysis). Thus, Coke is trading at a lower P/E relative to Pepsi and others in the industry: it is undervalued. This is an example of a line of reasoning you might offer when asked this question (the more thorough and insightful the reasoning, the better). Using some of the techniques discussed earlier as well as regular readings of the WSJ and other publications, will help you formulate real-world examples.

Visit the Vault Finance Career Channel at **www.vault.com/finance** — with insider firm profiles, message boards, the Vault Finance Job Board and more.

VAULT CAREER LIBRARY   53

Also, keep in mind that there are no absolute right answers for a question like this: If everyone in the market believed that a stock was undervalued, the price would go up and it wouldn't be undervalued anymore! What the interviewer is looking for is your chain of thought, your ability to communicate that convincingly, your interest in the markets and your preparation for the interview.

23. Walk me through the major items of an Income Statement.

Know all the items that go into the three major components: revenues, expenses and net income.

24. Which industries are you interested in? What are the multiples that you use for those industries?

As discussed, different industries use different multiples. Answering the first part of the question, pick an industry and know any major events that are happening. Next, if you claim interest in a certain industry, you better know how companies in the industry are commonly valued. (Don't answer the first question without knowing the answer to the second!)

25. Is 10 a high P/E ratio?

The answer to this or any question like this is, "it depends." P/E ratios are relative measurements, and in order to know whether a P/E ratio is high or low, we need to know the general P/E ratios of comparable companies. Generally, higher growth firms will have higher P/E ratios because their earnings will be low relative to their price, with the idea that the earnings will eventually grow more rapidly that the stock's price.

26. Describe a typical company's capital structure.

A company's capital structure is just what it sounds like: the structure of the capital that makes up the firm, or its debts and equity. Capital structure includes permanent, long-term financing of a company, including long-term debt, preferred stock and common stock, and retained earnings. The statement of a company's capital structure as expressed above reflects the order in which contributors to the capital structure are paid back, and the order in which they have claims on company's assets should it liquidate. Debt has first priority, then preferred stock holders, then common stock holders. Anything left over is put into the retained earnings account.

27. Value the following company given the following information (a written finance interview question):

	Year One	Year Two	Year Three	Year Four
EBIT	480.0	530.0	580.0	605.0
Depreciation	145.0	130.0	110.0	100.0
Capital Expenditures	160.0	140.0	130.0	110.0
Increase in Working Capital	25.0	20.0	15.0	12.0

Tax Rate (t)	40%
Book Value Debt (D)	1,200
Book Value Equity (E_{book})	1,500
Market Value Equity (E_{market})	1,800
Beta (historical) (β_L)	1.10
Long-term T-Bond rate (r_f)	8.0%
Long-term debt rate (r_D)	10.0%
Long-term growth rate (g)	4.0%
Long-term risk premium ($r_m - r_f$)	6.0%

Visit the Vault Finance Career Channel at **www.vault.com/finance** — with
insider firm profiles, message boards, the Vault Finance Job Board and more.

VAULT CAREER LIBRARY

55

Step 1: Figuring out free cash flows

Free cash flow to an all-equity firm = EBIT $(1 - t)$ + Depreciation - Capital Expenditures - Increase in Working Capital

Plugging in our data, our free cash flows look like this:

	Year One	Year Two	Year Three	Year Four
FCF	248.00	288.00	313.00	341.00

Step 2: Figuring out a discount rate

Remember that there are two ways to determine a discount rate. Let's begin with a discount rate for APV analysis:

APV

First, get β^U from the β^L of 1.50

$$\beta^U = \frac{\beta^L}{\left[1 + \dfrac{(1 - t)(D)}{E_{(market\ value)}}\right]}$$

$$\beta^U = \frac{1.10}{\left[1 + \dfrac{(1 - 0.40)(1,200)}{(1,800)}\right]}$$

$$r_e^U = r_f + \beta^U (r_m - r_f)$$

$$r_e^U = 0.08 + (0.79)(0.06) = \textbf{12.7\%}$$

The expected return on equity for an all-equity firm would be 12.7 percent. We will use this as the discount rate for the APV analysis.

WACC

Let's now look at the WACC method. For WACC, we need to know what the target (long-term) debt-to-capital ratio for this company is. Let's assume that it is 30 percent. That is, in the long run, this company expects to finance its projects with 30 percent debt and 70 percent equity.

First, we need to calculate ß^L

$$ß^L = ß^U\left[1 + (1-t)\frac{(D)}{(E)}\right]$$

$$ß^L = 0.79\left[1 + (1-0.40)\frac{(0.3)}{(0.7)}\right]$$

$$= \mathbf{0.993}$$

$$r_e^L = r_f + (ß^L)(0.06)$$

$$r_e^L = (0.08) + (0.993)(0.06) = \mathbf{13.95 \text{ or } 14.0\%}$$

Since our long-term debt rate is 10 percent, and our long-term debt is 30 percent, we can now calculate WACC.

$$\mathbf{WACC} = \frac{(E)}{(D+E)}(r_e^L) + \frac{(D)}{(D+E)}(1-t)(r_D)$$

$$\mathbf{WACC} = 0.7 \times 0.139 + 0.3 \times (1-0.4) \times 0.1$$

$$= \mathbf{0.1153 \text{ or } 11.53\%}$$

Step 3: Figuring out a terminal value

In figuring out a terminal value, first we assume that the company operates forever. Since we only have four years of cash flow, we need to put a value on all the cash flows after Year Four. Given that the Year Four cash flow is 341 and we expect it to grow at 5 percent a year, the value of all cash flows after Year Four (as of the end of Year Four) can be calculated with the Terminal Value formula of our choice (either APV or WACC).

APV

$$\text{TY FCF} = \frac{\text{FCF}_{10}\,(1 + g)}{(r_d - g)}$$

$$\text{TY FCF} = \frac{341(1 + 0.05)}{(0.127 - 0.05)} \qquad = \mathbf{4{,}650}$$

WACC

$$\text{TY FCF} = \frac{\text{FCF}_{10}\,(1 + g)}{(r_d - g)}$$

$$\text{TY FCF} = \frac{341(1 + 0.05)}{(0.1153 - 0.05)} \qquad = \mathbf{5{,}483}$$

Step 4: Figuring out the NPV of all the cash flows

Now we have to add up our cash flows

APV

	Year One	Year Two	Year Three	Year Four
FCF	248.00	288.00	313.00	341.00

Add terminal value = 4,650

FCF$_{\text{adjusted}}$	248.00	288.00	313.00	4,991

Using these cash flows, and our discount rate (r_e^u) of 12.7 percent, we can calculate the Net Present Value using the NPV formula.

$$\text{NPV} = \frac{\text{FCF}_1}{(1 + r_e^u)^1} + \frac{\text{FCF}_2}{(1 + r_e^u)^2} + \frac{\text{FCF}_3}{(1 + r_e^u)^3} + \frac{\text{FCF}_4}{(1 + r_e^u)^4}$$

$$\text{NPV} = \frac{248}{(1 + 0.127)} + \frac{288}{(1 + 0.127)^2} + \frac{313}{(1 + 0.127)^3} + \frac{4{,}991}{(1 + 0.127)^4}$$

$$\text{NPV} = 220 + 226.7 + 218.66 + 3{,}093.8 = \mathbf{3{,}759}$$

Let's add up the cash flows for the WACC method:

WACC

	Year One	Year Two	Year Three	Year Four
FCF	248.00	288.00	313.00	341.00

Add terminal value = 5,483

	Year One	Year Two	Year Three	Year Four
FCF$_{adjusted}$	248.00	288.00	313.00	5,824.15

$$R_E = R_E^L(WACC) = R_{WACC}$$

$$NPV = \frac{FCF_1}{(1+R_E)^1} + \frac{FCF_2}{(1+R_E)^2} + \frac{FCF_3}{(1+R_E)^3} + \frac{FCF_4}{(1+R_E)^4}$$

$$NPV = \frac{248}{(1+0.1153)} + \frac{288}{(1+0.1153)^2} + \frac{313}{(1+0.1153)^3} + \frac{5,824.15}{(1+0.1153)^4}$$

$$NPV = 222.36 + 231.53 + 225.6 + 3,764.1 = \mathbf{4,443.62}$$

Step 5: Putting it all together and figuring out the company's value

For WACC, we are done with our calculation – the value of the company is $4,443.62.

For APV, however since we've used unlevered numbers (numbers without debt involved), we need to add the present value of the interest tax shields we get from debt interest payments. We use the following formula to figure out the tax shield:

APV w/debt tax benefits = APV without debt tax benefits + DTS

DTS = APV without DTS X (Tax rate (t) X Long-term debt ratio)

If the company's long-term debt ratio is 30%:

DTS = 3759 X (.4 X .3)

DTS = $451

To summarize the results:

	APV	WACC
Discounted value of FCF	$3,759	$4,443
Value of tax shield	$451	
Total	$4,210	$4,443

EQUITY ANALYSIS AND PORTFOLIO MANAGEMENT

Investment Management and Portfolio Theory

Asset managers and portfolio managers (as well the job candidates interviewing for these positions) are expected to understand basic portfolio theory. This section covers the basics of portfolio theory. For more advanced concepts, read the *Vault Guide to Advanced Finance & Quantitative Interviews.*

Regardless of the type of portfolio he or she manages, the aim of every portfolio manager is the same: to achieve the highest rate of return possible given the asset class he or she is investing in while minimizing risk. As a portfolio manager, the type of risk you are allowed to assume depends on the type of assets or fund you are managing, but your job is still to keep the risk as low as you can while still achieving the expected returns.

Risk

In a nutshell, the riskiness of a portfolio is defined as the standard deviation of the portfolio's expected returns. Standard deviation is a measure of volatility. So, the more predictable a portfolio's returns are perceived to be, the less risky it is. Conversely, the less predictable a portfolio's returns are, the more risky the portfolio is. For example, a portfolio of stocks with relatively low revenue and high growth prospects, where the prices can move wildly from day to day, is a relatively "risky" portfolio.

A fact you need to face as a portfolio manager is that in order to receive an increased return from your investment portfolio, you need to accept an increased amount of risk. Keeping the assets in your portfolio in cash reduces the portfolio's risk, but it also reduces the potential return.

Portfolio risk vs. a single security's risk

Rather than look at risk at the individual security level, portfolio managers must constantly measure the risk of an entire portfolio. When an interviewer for a portfolio manager's job asks you whether you recommend adding a particular security to a portfolio, don't simply base your decision on the risk of the given security. Instead, consider how that security contributes to the overall risk of the portfolio. Using "correlation" is an effective technique for determining such portfolio-level risk.

Correlation

The tendency for two investments in a portfolio to move together in price under the same circumstances is called "correlation." If two investments have a strong positive correlation, they tend to move together. For example, the stocks of Microsoft and Intel have a strong positive correlation. Both are impacted by the demand for technology. Therefore, you can expect the stocks of these two companies to generally move in the same direction.

If two stocks have a strong negative correlation, they will tend to move in opposite directions. For example, high fuel prices might be good for oil companies, but bad for airlines who need to buy the fuel. As a result, you might expect that the stocks of companies in these two industries to move in opposite directions. These two industries have a negative correlation. You'll get better diversification in your portfolio if you own one airline and one oil company, rather than two oil companies. However, your returns may be lower.

Note that the correlation between two things can be measured by a number called a correlation coefficient. The correlation coefficient between two securities can range from -1 (i.e., a perfect negative correlation) to +1 (i.e., a perfect positive correlation). A correlation coefficient of zero implies that the two assets have no correlation with one another. You can calculate the correlation coefficient between two securities using a formula or a financial software program, though if you work at an investment bank you can usually just look up this number.

Diversification

When the term "diversification" is used, it usually means building a portfolio that includes securities from different asset classes, like stocks and bonds. However, realize that this is the case precisely because bonds often tend to do well when stocks don't (i.e., they have a low correlation). Another way to diversify a portfolio is to buy securities in the same asset class that are not affected by the same variables and that therefore also have a low correlation (think oil and airlines). Conversely, a portfolio of securities with a strong positive correlation will be relatively undiversified and therefore more risky, but may garner higher returns.

Visit the Vault Finance Career Channel at **www.vault.com/finance** — with
insider firm profiles, message boards, the Vault Finance Job Board and more.

VAULT CAREER LIBRARY

63

Risk level of a portfolio with two securities:

Type of Correlation	Correlation Coefficient	Risk Level	Example
Securities have a **strong positive** correlation	Close to 1	High	Microsoft and Intel
Securities have a **weak** or zero correlation	Close to zero	Medium	Microsoft and H&R Block
Securities have a **strong negative** correlation	Close to -1	Low	Exxon and Federal Express

Stock Analysis and Stock Picking

Technical analysis vs. fundamental analysis

Technical analysis involves looking at charts and patterns associated with a stock's historical price movements to try to profit from predictable patterns, regardless of fundamentals such as revenue growth or expense trends. While many on Wall Street look down upon technical analysis (and it is rarely taught at business schools), some Wall Street traders still rely on it or use it in conjunction with fundamental analysis to decide whether and when to buy and sell.

In contrast, fundamental analysis of a stock (or other security) involves using financial analysis to analyze the company's underlying business, such as sales growth, its balance sheet, etc., (its "fundamentals") to decide whether and when to buy and sell.

For the most part, your interviewers will be looking for your skills in fundamental analysis, though if you're interviewing for a trading position your interviewer might expect you to have some familiarity with technical analysis.

Stock valuation techniques

The most common forms of fundamental analysis involve the traditional valuation techniques (DCF, multiples analysis) as well as the various accounting and financial statement analyses that are covered in the Valuation Techniques chapter. For investment management interviews, you should have a strong command for these techniques for valuing individual stocks.

Financial ratios

Another important form of stock analysis is Ratio Analysis, which involves looking at a company's various financial ratios and how they have changed over time to spot trends or trouble spots in the company's operations. A financial ratio by itself doesn't necessary tell you very much. More important is comparing how a company's financial ratios are changing from one quarter to the next, and how they compare a company's financial ratios with other companies in its industry.

Below are the most common ratios used in finance to analyze companies. Particularly if you are interviewing for investment management, equity research or similar finance positions, you may be asked questions about how to calculate common financial ratios and what they signify.

Solvency Ratios		
Quick Ratio	$$\frac{\text{Cash + Accounts Receivable}}{\text{Total Current Liabilities}}$$	Shows the amount of liquid assets (i.e., cash or assets that can be quickly converted to cash) on hand to cover current debts
Current Ratio	$$\frac{\text{Total Current Assets}}{\text{Total Current Liabilities}}$$	Similar to the Quick Ratio, but broader, since it includes less liquid assets that may be used to cover current debts
Cash Ratio (also called Liquidity Ratio)	$$\frac{\text{Cash}}{\text{Total Current Liabilities}}$$	Shows the cash on hand to cover current liabilities
Debt to Equity	$$\frac{\text{Debt}}{\text{Equity}}$$	Shows the amount of shareholders' equity available to cover debts
Current Liabilities to Inventory	$$\frac{\text{Total Current Liabilities}}{\text{Inventory}}$$	Shows how much a company can rely on unsold inventory to cover debts
Total Liabilities to Net Worth	$$\frac{\text{Total Liabilities}}{\text{Net Worth}}$$	Similar to the debt to equity ratio, but broader since it includes all the company's liabilities, not just debt

Visit the Vault Finance Career Channel at **www.vault.com/finance** — with insider firm profiles, message boards, the Vault Finance Job Board and more.

VAULT CAREER LIBRARY

65

Efficiency Ratios		
Collection Period (also called Day Sales Outstanding)	$\dfrac{\text{Accounts Receivable}}{\text{Sales X 365}}$	Shows the average amount of time it takes a company to collect from customers
Inventory Turnover (also called Inventory Utilization Ratio)	$\dfrac{\text{Sales}}{\text{Inventory}}$	Shows how quickly a company is selling its inventory
Sales to Assets	$\dfrac{\text{Sales}}{\text{Total Assets}}$	Measures how efficiently a company is using its assets to generate sales
Sales to Net Working Capital	$\dfrac{\text{Sales}}{\text{Net Working Capital}}$	Shows a company's ability to use short-term assets and liabilities to generate revenue
Gross Profit Margin (also called Return on Sales)	$\dfrac{\text{Gross Profit}}{\text{Sales}}$	A measure of efficiency — shows profits earned per dollar of sales
Return on Assets	$\dfrac{\text{Net Profit After Taxes}}{\text{Total Assets}}$	Shows profits relative to a company's assets
Return on Equity (also called Return on Net Worth)	$\dfrac{\text{Net Profit After Taxes}}{\text{Net Worth}}$	Shows profits relative to equity

You can use these ratios to ascertain the health of a company. For example, a higher current ratio is better; a company's position is improving when the collection period declines. Here's a quick chart that explains whether a higher or lower ratio is better.

Ratio	Good Trend	Bad Trend
Quick Ratio	Rising	Falling
Current Ratio	Rising	Falling
Cash Ratio	Rising	Falling
Debt to Equity	Falling	Rising
Current Liabilities to Inventory	Falling	Rising
Total Liabilities to Net Worth	Falling	Rising
Collection Period	Falling	Rising
Inventory Turnover	Rising	Falling

Ratio	Good Trend	Bad Trend
Sales to Assets	Rising	Falling
Sales to Net Working Capital	Rising	Falling
Gross Profit Margin	Rising	Falling
Return on Assets	Rising	Falling
Return on Equity	Rising	Falling

Questions

1. If you add a risky stock into a portfolio that is already risky, how is the overall portfolio risk affected?

A. It becomes riskier

B. It becomes less risky

C. Overall risk is unaffected

D. It depends on the stock's risk relative to that of the portfolio

Answer: D. In modern portfolio theory, if you add a risky stock into a portfolio that is already risky, the resulting portfolio may be more or less risky than before.

A portfolio's overall risk is determined not just by the riskiness of its individual positions, but also by how those positions are correlated with each other. For example, a portfolio with two high-tech stocks might at first glance be considered risky, but if those two stocks tends to move in opposite directions, then the riskiness of the portfolio overall could be significantly lower. So the risk effect of adding a new stock to an existing portfolio depends on how that stock correlates with the other stocks in the portfolio.

2. Put the following portfolios consisting of 2 stocks in order from the least risky to the most risky and explain why

A. A portfolio of a cable television company stock and an oil company stock

B. A portfolio of an airline company stock and a cruise ship company stock

C. A portfolio of an airline company stock and an oil company stock.

Answer: Least risky: C. Then A. B is the most risky.

Visit the Vault Finance Career Channel at **www.vault.com/finance** — with
insider firm profiles, message boards, the Vault Finance Job Board and more.

VAULT CAREER LIBRARY

67

The least risky portfolio is the one where the two securities have a strong negative correlation. Stocks with a strong negative correlation tend to move in the opposite direction under the same circumstances. Therefore, the value of the portfolio will remain relatively stable over time, making the portfolio less risky. In this question, since high fuel prices might be good for oil companies, but bad for airlines who need to buy the fuel, you would expect that the stocks of companies in these two industries to move in opposite directions. These two industries have a strong negative correlation and portfolio C is the least risky.

Portfolio B is the most risky because the stocks of airline companies and cruise ship companies have a strong positive correlation: they tend to move in the same direction under the same circumstances. For example, after the September 11 terrorist attacks all travel related businesses suffered from sharply lower demand. A portfolio of two securities with a strong positive correlation will be the most risky.

Portfolio A is in the middle because we would expect cable TV stocks and oil stocks to have a weak correlation. A weak correlation (correlation coefficient of around 0) means that the two securities generally do not move in the same direction under the same circumstances.

3. How do you calculate a company's Days Sales Outstanding?

Average Accounts Receivable/ Sales x 365 days

Note: The average accounts receivable for any period can be approximated by:

(Ending accounts receivable + beginning accounts receivable) ÷ 2

4. How do you calculate a company's Current Ratio?

Current assets (cash, accounts receivable, etc) / Current liabilities (accounts payable and other short-term liabilities)

A high current ratio indicates that a company has enough cash (and assets they can quickly turn into cash, like accounts receivable) to cover its immediate payment requirements on liabilities.

5. Gotham Energy just released second quarter financial results. Looking at its balance sheet you calculate that it's Current Ratio went from 1.5 to 1.2. Does this make you more or less likely to buy the stock?

Less likely. This means that the company is less able to cover its immediate liabilities with cash on hand and other current assets than it was last quarter.

6. Xeron Software Corporation's days sales outstanding have gone from 58 days to 42 days. Does this make you more or less likely to issue a Buy rating on the stock?

More likely. When the company's days sales outstanding (DSOs) decreases, it means the company is able to collect money from its customers faster. In other words, Xeron's customers went from taking an average of 58 days to pay their bills to 42 days. All things being equal, having faster paying customers is almost always a good thing. Of course, one caveat is that you want to make sure Xeron didn't achieve this by imposing much tighter credit terms on its customers and therefore. But if the company's sales grew at the same time its DSOs decreased, then as a research analyst or trader you'll be more likely to want to buy the stock.

Visit the Vault Finance Career Channel at **www.vault.com/finance** — with insider firm profiles, message boards, the Vault Finance Job Board and more.

VAULT CAREER LIBRARY

69

STOCKS

A Remedial Lesson

What does the "Inc." after the names of many companies mean? In short, Inc. stands for "incorporated," a legal term that makes an entity a legal company. There are many forms of incorporation from which a company can choose. With the help of a lawyer, a company files papers/applications in court to define itself as one of these forms. A company can be incorporated as a C Corp, an S Corp, an LLC (Limited Liability Corporation), or a partnership. There are different rules of ownership for each of these forms, which determine in part how a company pays out profits, is taxed, and so on.

The incorporation of a company can be regarded as its birth. And when a company is born, it has equity. This equity is also referred to as stock, and refers to ownership in a company. Most people unfamiliar with the finance world equate stock with the running tickers in the pits of Wall Street trading floors, and other symbols of publicly traded stock. You should realize that companies do not have to be publicly traded in order to have stock – they just have to be incorporated and owned.

Equity vs. Debt (Stocks vs. Bonds)

Companies are traditionally financed through a combination of debt and equity. Equity, or ownership stake, is more volatile as its value fluctuates with the value of the firm. The equity of a company is represented by securities called stocks. Here, when we refer to stock, we are referring to common stock, or stock without a guaranteed return (as opposed to prefered stock).

Equity has a book value – this is a strictly defined value that can be calculated from the company's Balance Sheet. It also has a market value. The market value of equity or stock for a publicly traded firm can be found in *The Wall Street Journal* or any of the stock quote services available today. (Market value of a company's equity can be understood with the simple formula: stock price x number of shares outstanding [or common stock outstanding] = market value of equity.) The market value of a private company can be estimated using the valuation techniques discussed in the valuation section of this guide. However, any method used to measure either the book value or market value of a company depends on highly volatile factors such as performance of the company, the industry and the market as a whole – and is thus highly volatile itself. Investors can make lots of money based on their equity investment decisions and the subsequent changing value of those stocks after they are bought.

The other component of the financing of a company is debt, which is represented by securities called bonds. (In its simplest form, debt is issued when investors loan money to a company at a given interest rate.) Typically, banks and large financial institutions originate debt. The returns for debt investors are assured in the form of interest on the debt. Sometimes, the market value of the debt changes (see chapter on bonds), but bond prices usually do not change as drastically as stock prices. On the downside, bonds also have lower expected returns than stocks. U.S. Treasury bonds, for example, can provide returns of 5 to 7 percent a year or so, while volatile stocks may rise 10 percent in a single day. On the other hand, bonds usually have less downside risk than stock. Though they won't post big gains, U.S. Treasury bonds won't lose 10 percent of their value in a single day, either.

A simple analogy of how debt and equity make up financing for a company is to consider how most people buy homes. Homebuyers generally start with a down payment, which is a payment on the equity of the house. Then, the homebuyer makes mortgage payments that are a combination of debt (the interest on the mortgage) and equity (the principal payments). Initially, a homebuyer generally pays primarily interest (debt), before gradually buying larger and large portions of the principal (equity). Common stock and debt are the two extremes in the continuum of the forms of investment in a company.

In the middle of the continuum is preferred stock. One type of preferred stock is referred to as convertible preferred. If the preferred stock is convertible, it can be converted into common stock as prescribed in the initial issuance of the preferred stock. Like bondholders, holders of preferred stock are assured an interest-like return – also referred to as the preferred stock's dividend. (A dividend is a payment made to stockholders, usually quarterly, that is intended to distribute some of the company's profits to shareholders.)

The other key difference between preferred and common stock comes into play when a company goes bankrupt. In what is referred to as the seniority of creditors, the debt holders have first claim on the assets of the firm if the company becomes insolvent. Preferred shareholders are next in line, while the common stock shareholders bring up the rear. This isn't just a matter of having to wait in line longer if you are a common stock shareholder. If the bondholders and owners of preferred stock have claims that exceed the value of the assets of a bankrupt company, the common stock shareholders won't see a dime.

There is a tax advantage for corporations who invest in preferred stock rather than in bonds for other companies. Corporate investors are taxed for only 30 percent of the dividends they receive on preferred stock. On the other hand, 100 percent of the interest payments on bonds paid to corporate investors are taxed. This tax rule comes in handy when structuring mergers.

Seniority of creditors:

1. Bondholders
2. Preferred stockholders
3. Common stockholders

Stock Terminology

Of course, a company's commitment to its stock doesn't end after the issuance of shares. Companies communicate with shareholders regarding the firm's past revenues, expenses and profits and the future of the business. There are also ways a company can manage their shares once the stock is on the open market to maximize shareholder value, the company's reputation and the company's future ability to raise funds. Here are several concepts and terms you'll need to be familiar with when you study stocks and how public companies manage their shares.

Dividends

Dividends are paid to many shareholders of common stock (and preferred stock). However, the directors cannot pay any dividends to the common stock shareholders until they have paid all outstanding dividends to the preferred stockholders. The incentive for company directors to issue dividends is that companies in industries that are particularly dividend sensitive have better market valuations if they regularly issue dividends. Issuing regular dividends is a signal to the market that the company is doing well.

Unlike bonds, however, the company directors decide when to pay the dividend on preferred stock. In contrast, if a company fails to meet bond payments as scheduled, the bondholders can force the company into Chapter 11 bankruptcy. (Bankruptcy filing in court comes in two categories: Chapter

7 and Chapter 11. If a Chapter 11 bankruptcy filing is approved, the court puts a stay order on all interest payments – management is given a period of protection during which it can clean up its financial mess and try to get the house marching toward profitability. If the management fails to do so within the given time, there can be a Chapter 7 bankruptcy filing, when the assets of the company are liquidated.) This action, in theory, wipes out the value of the company's equity.

Stock splits

As a company grows in value, it sometimes splits its stock so that the price does not become absurdly high. This enables the company to maintain the liquidity of the stock. If The Coca-Cola Company had never split its stock, the price of one share bought when the company's stock was first offered would be worth millions of dollars. If that were the case, buying and selling one share would be a very crucial decision. This would adversely affect a stock's liquidity (that is, its ability to be freely traded on the market). In theory, splitting the stock neither creates nor destroys value. However, splitting the stock is generally received as a positive signal to the market; therefore, the share price typically rises when a stock split is announced.

Stock buybacks

Often you will hear that a company has announced that it will buy back its own stock. Such an announcement is usually followed by an increase in the stock price. Why does a company buy back its stock? And why does its price increase after?

The reason behind the price increase is fairly complex, and involves three major reasons. The first has to do with the influence of earnings per share on market valuation. Many investors believe that if a company buys back shares, and the number of outstanding shares decreases, the company's earnings per share goes up. If the P/E (price to earnings-per-share ratio) stays stable, investors reason, the price should go up. Thus investors drive the stock price up in anticipation of increased earnings per share.

The second reason has to do with the signaling effect. This reason is simple to understand, and largely explains why a company buys back stock. No one understands the health of the company better than its senior managers. No one is in a better position to judge what will happen to the future performance of the company. So if a company decides to buy back stock (i.e., decides to invest in its own stock), these managers must believe that the stock price is undervalued and will rise (or so most observers would believe). This is the signal company management sends to the market, and the market pushes the stock up in anticipation.

The third reason the stock price goes up after a buyback can be understood in terms of the debt tax shield (a concept used in valuation methods). When a company buys back stock, its net debt goes up (net debt = debt - cash). Thus the debt tax shield associated with the company goes up and the valuation rises (see APV valuation).

New stock issues

The reverse of a stock buyback is when a company issues new stock, which usually is followed by a drop in the company's stock price. As with stock buybacks, there are three main reasons for this movement. First, investors believe that issuing new shares dilutes earnings. That is, issuing new stock increases the number of outstanding shares, which decreases earnings per share, which – given a stable P/E ratio – decreases the share price. (Of course, the issuing of new stock will presumably be used in a way that will increase earnings, and thus the earnings per share figure won't necessarily decrease, but because investors believe in earnings dilution, they often drive stock prices down) .

There is also the signaling effect. In other words, investors may ask why the company's senior managers decided to issue equity rather than debt to meet their financing requirements. Surely, investors may believe, management must believe that the valuation of their stock is high (possibly inflated) and that by issuing stock they can take advantage of this high price.

Finally, if the company believes that the project for which they need money will definitely be successful, it would have issued debt, thus keeping all of the upside of the investment within the firm rather than distributing it away in the form of additional equity. The stock price also drops because of debt tax shield reasons. Because cash is flushed into the firm through the sale of equity, the net debt decreases. As net debt decreases, so does the associated debt tax shield.

Questions

1. What kind of stocks would you issue for a startup?

A startup typically has more risk than a well-established firm. The kind of stocks that one would issue for a startup would be those that protect the downside of equity holders while giving them upside. Hence the stock issued may be a combination of common stock, preferred stock and debt notes with warrants (options to buy stock).

2. When should a company buy back stock?

When it believes the stock is undervalued, has extra cash, and believes it can make money by investing in itself. This can happen in a variety of situations. For example, if a company has suffered some decreased earnings because of an inherently cyclical industry (such as the semiconductor industry), and believes its stock price is unjustifiably low, it will buy back its own stock. On other occasions, a company will buy back its stock if investors are driving down the price precipitously. In this situation, the company is attempting to send a signal to the market that it is optimistic that its falling stock price is not justified. It's saying: "We know more than anyone else about our company. We are buying our stock back. Do you really think our stock price should be this low?"

3. Is the dividend paid on common stock taxable to shareholders? Preferred stock? Is it tax deductible for the company?

The dividend paid on common stock is taxable on two levels in the U.S. First, it is taxed at the firm level, as a dividend comes out from the net income after taxes (i.e., the money has been taxed once already). The shareholders are then taxed for the dividend as ordinary income (O.I.) on their personal income tax. Dividend for preferred stock is treated as an interest expense and is tax-free at the corporate level.

4. When should a company issue stock rather than debt to fund its operations?

There are several reasons for a company to issue stock rather than debt. If the company believes its stock price is inflated it can raise money (on very good terms) by issuing stock. Second, if the projects for which the money is being raised may not generate predictable cash flows in the immediate future, it may issue stock. A simple example of this is a startup company. The owners of startups generally will issue stock rather than take on debt because their ventures will probably not generate predictable cash flows, which is needed to make regular debt payments, and also so that the risk of the venture is diffused among the company's shareholders. A third reason for a company to raise money by selling equity is if it wants to change its debt-to-equity ratio. This ratio in part determines a company's bond rating. If a company's bond rating is poor because it is struggling with large debts, the company may decide to issue equity to pay down the debt.

5. Why would an investor buy preferred stock?

1) An investor that wants the upside potential of equity but wants to minimize risk would buy preferred stock. The investor would receive steady interest-like payments (dividends) from the preferred stock that are more assured than the dividends from common stock. 2) The preferred stock owner gets a superior right to the company's assets should the company go bankrupt. 3) A corporation would invest in preferred stock because the dividends on preferred stock are taxed at a lower rate than the interest rates on bonds.

6. Why would a company distribute its earnings through dividends to common stockholders?

Regular dividend payments are signals that a company is healthy and profitable. Also, issuing dividends can attract investors (shareholders). Finally, a company may distribute earnings to shareholders if it lacks profitable investment opportunities.

7. What stocks do you like?

This is a question often asked of those applying for all equity (sales & trading, research, etc.) positions. (Applicants for investment banking and trading positions, as well as investment management positions, have also reported receiving this question.) If you're interviewing for one of these positions, you should prepare to talk about a couple of stocks you believe are good buys and some that you don't. This is also a question asked of undergraduate finance candidates to gauge their level of interest in finance.

8. What did the S&P 500 close at yesterday?

Another question designed to make sure that a candidate is sincerely interested in finance. This question (and others like it – "What's the Dow at now?" "What's the yield on the Long Bond?") can be expected especially of those looking for sales and trading positions.

9. Why did the stock price of XYZ company decrease yester announced increased quarterly earnings?

A couple of possible explanations: 1) the entire market was down, (or the sector to which XYZ belongs was down), or 2) even though XYZ announced increased earnings, the Street was expecting earnings to increase even more.

10. Can you tell me about a recent IPO that you have followed?

Read *The Wall Street Journal* and stay current with recent offerings.

11. What is your investing strategy?

Different investors have different strategies. Some look for undervalued stocks, others for stocks with growth potential and yet others for stocks with steady performance. A strategy could also be focused on the long-term or short-term, and be more risky or less risky. Whatever your investing strategy is, you should be able to articulate these attributes.

12. How has your portfolio performed in the last five years?

If you are applying for an investment management firm as an MBA, you'd better have a good answer for this one. If you don't have a portfolio, start a mock one using Yahoo! Finance or other tools. Also, if you think you are going to say it has outperformed the S&P each year, you better be well prepared to explain why you think this happened.

13. If you read that a given mutual fund has achieved 50 percent returns last year, would you invest in it?

You should look for more information, as past performance is not necessarily an indicator of future results. How has the overall market done? How did it do in the years before? Why did it give 50 percent returns last year? Can that strategy be expected to work continuously over the next five to 10 years? You need to look for answers to these questions before making a decision.

14. You are on the board of directors of a company and own a significant chunk of the company. The CEO, in his annual presentation, states that the company's stock is doing well, as it has gone up 20 percent in the last 12 months. Is the company's stock in fact doing well?

Another trick stock question that you should not answer too quickly. First, ask what the Beta of the company is. (Remember, the Beta represents the volatility of the stock with respect to the market.) If the Beta is 1 and the market (i.e. the Dow Jones Industrial Average) has gone up 35 percent, the company actually has not done too well compared to the broader market.

15. Which do you think has higher growth potential, a stock that is currently trading at $2 or a stock that is trading at $60?

This question tests your fundamental understanding of a stock's value. The short answer to the question is, "It depends." While at first glance it may appear that the stock with the lower price has more room for growth, price does not tell the entire picture. Suppose the $2 stock has 1 billion shares outstanding. That means it has $2 billion market cap, hardly a small cap stock. On the flip side, if the $60 stock has 20,000 shares gives it a market cap of $1,200,000, and hence it is extremely small and is probably seen as having higher growth potential. Generally, high growth potential has little to do with a stock's price, and has more to do with it's operations and revenue prospects.

16. What do you think is happening with ABC stock?

Expect to be asked this question if you say you like to follow a given sector like technology or pharmaceuticals. Interviewers will test you to see how well you know your industry. In case you don't know that stock, admit it, and offer to describe a stock in that sector that you like or have been following.

17. Where do you think the DJIA will be in three months and six months – and why?

Nobody knows the answer to this one. However, you should at least have some thoughts on the subject and be able to articulate why you take your stance. If you have been following the performance of major macroeconomic indicators (which will be reviewed in the next section), you can state your case well.

18. Why do some stocks rise so much on the first day of trading after their IPO and others don't? How is that money left on the table?

By "money left on the table," bankers mean that the company could have successfully completed the offering at a higher price, and that the difference in valuation thus goes to initial investors rather than the company. Why this happens is not easy to predict from responses received from investors during roadshows. Moreover, if the stock rises a lot the first day it is good publicity for the firm. But in many ways it is money left on the table because the company could have sold the same stock in its initial public offering at a higher price. However, bankers must honestly value a company and its stock over the long-term, rather than simply trying to guess what the market will do. Even if a stock trades up significantly initially, a banker looking at the long-term would expect the stock to come down, as long as the market eventually correctly values it.

19. What is insider trading and why is it illegal?

Undergraduates may get this question as feelers of their general knowledge of the finance industry. Insider trading describes the illegal activity of buying or selling stock based on information that is not public information. The law against insider trading exists to prevent those with privileged information (company execs, I-bankers and lawyers) from using this information to make a tremendous amount of money unfairly.

20. Who is a more senior creditor, a bondholder or stockholder?

The bondholder is always more senior. Stockholders (including those who own preferred stock) must wait until bondholders are paid during a bankruptcy before claiming company assets.

Visit the Vault Finance Career Channel at **www.vault.com/finance** — with
insider firm profiles, message boards, the Vault Finance Job Board and more.

VAULT CAREER LIBRARY   **81**

BONDS AND INTEREST RATES

A Remedial Lesson

A bond is a borrowing arrangement through which the borrower (or seller of a bond) issues or sells an IOU document (the bond) to the investor (or buyer of the bond). The arrangement obligates the borrower to make specified payments to the bondholder on agreed-upon dates. For example, if you purchase a five-year U.S. Treasury note, the U.S. government is borrowing money from you for a period of five years. For this service, the government will pay you interest at the T-bill rate (the interest) and return the amount it borrowed (the principal) at the end of five years. Meanwhile, if you choose not to keep the bond until it matures, you can sell the bond in the market for the current value of the future interest payments and the end principal. Different types of organizations can issue bonds: companies like Ford Motor or Procter & Gamble, and municipal organizations, like counties and states.

Bond Terminology

Before going any further in our discussion of bonds, we will introduce several terms you should be familiar with.

- **Par value or face value of a bond:** This is the total amount the bond issuer will commit to pay back at the end of the bond maturity period (when the bond expires).

- **Coupon payments:** The payments of interest that the bond issuer makes to the bondholder. These are often specified in terms of coupon rates. The coupon rate is the bond coupon payment divided by the bond's par value.

- **Bond price:** The price the bondholder (i.e. the lender) pays the bond issuer (i.e. the borrower) to hold the bond (to have a claim on the cash flows documented on the bond).

- **Default risk:** The risk that the company issuing the bond may go bankrupt, and default on its loans.

- **Default premium:** The difference between the promised yields on a corporate bond and the yield on an otherwise identical government bond. In theory, the difference compensates the bondholder for the corporation's default risk.

- **Credit ratings:** Bonds are rated by credit agencies (Moody's, Standard & Poor's), which examine a company's financial situation, outstanding debt, and other factors to determine the risk of default. Companies guard their credit ratings closely, because the higher the rating, the easier they can raise money and the lower the interest rate.

- **Investment grade bonds:** These bonds have high credit ratings, and pay a relatively low rate of interest.

- **Junk bonds:** Also known as high yield bonds, these bonds have poor credit ratings, and pay a relatively high rate of interest.

- **U.S. Treasury bills, notes, and bonds:** Bills mature in one year or less, notes in two to 10 years., and bonds in 30 years. (The 30-year U.S. Treasury bond is also called The Long Bond.)

To illustrate how a bond works, let's look at an 8% coupon, 30-year maturity bond with a par value of $1,000, paying 60 coupon payments of $40 each.

Let's illustrate this bond with the following schematic:

Coupon rate   = 8%

Par value   = $1,000

Therefore the coupon =   8% x $1,000 = $80 per year

Because this bond is a semiannual coupon, the payments are for $40 every six months. We can also say that the semiannual coupon rate is 4 percent.

Since the bond's time to maturity is 30 years, there are total of 30 x 2 = 60 semiannual payments.

At the end of Year 30, the bondholder receives the last semiannual payment of $40 dollars plus the principal of $1,000.

Pricing Bonds

The question now is, how much is a bond worth?

The price of a bond is the net present value of all future cash flows expected from that bond. (Recall net present value from our discussion on valuation.)

$$\text{Bond Value} = \sum_{t=1}^{T} \left(\frac{\text{Coupon}}{(1+r)^t} \right) + \frac{\text{Par Value}}{(1+r)^T}$$

Here:

r   =   Discount rate

t   =   Interval (for example, 6 months)

T   =   Total payments

First, we must ask what discount rate should be used? Remember from our discussion of valuation techniques that discount rate for a cash flow for a given period should be able to account for the risk associated with the cash flow for that period. In practice, there will be different discount rates for cash flows occurring in different periods. However, for the sake of simplicity, we will assume that the discount rate is the same as the interest rate on the bond.

So, what is the price of the bond described earlier? From the equation above we get:

$$\text{Price} = \sum_{t=1}^{T} \left(\frac{\$40}{(1+.04)^t} \right) + \frac{\$1000}{(1+.04)^{60}}$$

Calculating the answer for this equation is complex. Luckily, this can be solved using a financial calculator. It might be worth noting that the first term of this equation is the present value of an annuity with fixed payments, $40 every 6 months for 30 years in this example. Also, there are Present Value tables available that simplify the calculations. In this case, the interest rate is 4 percent and T is 60. Using the Present Value tables we get

= $904.94 + $95.06

= $1000

Also, if we look at the bond price equation closely, we see that the bond price depends on the interest rate. If the interest rate is higher, the bond price is lower and vice versa. This is a fundamental rule that should be understood and remembered.

The Yield to Maturity (YTM) is the measure of the average rate of return that will be earned on a bond if it is bought now and held until maturity. To calculate this, we need the information on bond price, coupon rate and par value of the bond.

Example: Suppose an 8% coupon, 30-year bond is selling at $1,276.76. What average rate of return would be earned if you purchase the bond at this price?

To answer this question, we must find the interest rate at which the present value of the bond payments equals the bond price. This is the rate that is consistent with the observed price of the bond. Therefore, we solve for r in the following equation.

$$\$1276.76 = \sum_{t=1}^{60}\left(\frac{\$40}{(1+r)^t}\right) + \frac{\$1{,}000}{(1+r)^{60}}$$

This equation can be solved using a financial calculator; in completing the calculation we see that the bond's yield to maturity is 3 percent semi-annually.

Visit the Vault Finance Career Channel at **www.vault.com/finance** — with insider firm profiles, message boards, the Vault Finance Job Board and more.

VAULT CAREER LIBRARY

87

Holding Period Return (HPR)

The income earned over a period as a percentage of the bond price at the start of the period, assuming that the bond is sold at the end of the period.

Example: Let's take a 30-year bond, with an $80 coupon, purchased for $1000 with a Yield to Maturity (YTM) of 8 percent. Say at the end of the year, the bond price increases to $1,050. Then the YTM will go below 8 percent, but the HPR will be higher than 8 percent and is given by:

$$ HPR = \frac{(\$80) + (\$1,050 - \$1,000)}{\$1,000} = 13\% $$

Callable bonds

For the sake of simplification in our earlier discussions, we assumed that the discount rate was equal to the interest rate, and that the interest rate was constant at the coupon rate. However, in the real world, this is not always the case.

If the interest rate falls, bond prices can rise substantially, due to the concept of opportunity cost of investments.

We'll illustrate mathmatically why this happens with an example. Let's say a company has a bond outstanding. It took $810.71 and promised to make the coupon payments as described above, at $40 every six months. Let's say the market interest rates dropped after a while (below 8 percent). According to the bond document, the company is still expected to pay the coupon at a rate of 8 percent.

If the interest rates were to drop in this manner, the company would be paying a coupon rate much higher than the market interest rate today. In such a situation, the company may want to buy the bond back so that it is not committed to paying large coupon payments in the future. This is referred to as calling the bond. However, an issuer can only call a bond if the bond was originally issued as a callable bond. The risk that a bond will be called is reflected in the bond's price. The yield calculated up to the period when the bond is called back is referred to as the yield to call.

Zero coupon bonds

This type of bond offers no coupon or interest payments to the bondholder. The only payment the zero coupon bondholder receives is the payment of the bond face value upon maturity. The returns on their coupon bonds must be obtained by paying a lower initial price than their face value for them. These bonds are priced at a considerable discount to par value.

Forward rates

These are agreed-upon interest rates for a bond to be issued in the future. For example, the one year forward rate for a five-year U.S. Treasury note represents the interest forward rate on a five-year T-note that will be issued one year from now (and that will mature six years from now). This "forward" rate changes daily just like the rates of already-issued bonds. It is essentially based on the market's expectation of what the interest rate a year from now will be, and can be calculated using the rates of current bonds.

The Fed and Interest Rates

The Federal Reserve Board has broad responsibility for the health of the U.S. financial system. In this role, the Fed sets the margin requirements on stocks and options, and regulates bank lending to securities market participants.

The Fed also has the responsibility of formulating the nation's monetary policy. In determining the monetary policy of the nation, the Fed manipulates the money supply to effect the macroeconomy. When the Fed increases the money supply going into the economy, the monetary policy set by the Fed is said to be expansionary. This encourages investment and subsequently increases consumption demand. In the long run, however, an expansionary policy can lead to higher prices and inflation. Therefore, it is the Fed's responsibility to maintain a proper balance and prevent the economy from both hyperinflation or recession.

The Fed uses several tools to regulate the money supply. The Fed can 1) use its check writing capabilities, using open market operations 2) raise or lower the interest rates, or 3) manipulate the reserve requirements for various banks to control the money flow and thereby the interest rate.

Visit the Vault Finance Career Channel at **www.vault.com/finance** — with
insider firm profiles, message boards, the Vault Finance Job Board and more.
VAULT CAREER LIBRARY   **89**

Let's look at these tools one by one:

1. Open market operations

The Fed can "write a check" to buy securities and thereby increase the money supply to do such things as buy back government bonds in the market. Unlike the rest of us, the Fed doesn't have to pay the money for a check it has written. As we will see, an increase in the country's money supply stimulates the economy. Likewise, if the Fed sells securities, the money paid for them leaves the money supply and slows the economy.

2. Changing interest rates

The Fed can raise or lower interest rates by changing: (a) the discount rate (the interest rate the Fed charges banks on short-term loans), and/or (b) the Federal Funds rate (or Fed Funds rate), the rate banks charge each other on short-term loans. When the Fed raises or lowers interest rates, banks usually quickly follow by raising or lowering their prime rate (the rate banks charge on loans to its most creditworthy customers). A reduction of the interest rate signals an expansionary monetary policy. Why? Because by reducing the interest of its loans to banks, the Fed allows banks to lend out money at lower rates. More businesses and individuals are willing to take out loans, thus pouring more money into the economy.

3. Reserve requirements

All banks that are members of the Federal Reserve System are required to maintain a minimum balance in a reserve account with the Fed. The amount of this minimum balance depends on the total deposits of the bank's customers. These minimum deposits are referred to as "reserve requirements." Lowering the reserve requirements for various banks has the same expansionary effect. This move allows banks to make more loans with the deposits it has and thereby stimulates the economy by increasing the money supply.

But why does an increase in money supply stimulate the economy? An increase in the money supply usually results in investors having too much money in their portfolios, which leads them to buy more stocks and bonds and gives them more discretionary income. In part, this action increases the demand for bonds, drives up bond prices, and thereby reduces interest rates. More money available also increases demand for stocks and real estate. This availability leads to higher investments and greater demand for goods.

The Fed and Inflation

Inflation is the rise of prices over time – it is why over the long-term, we are guaranteed to hear and (sorry, it's true) speak phrases like: "When I was your age, a can of Coke was only 50 cents." Prices rise over time becasue of increases in population and resultant demands for products.

Inflation directly affects interest rates. Consider this: If lending money is healthy for the economy because it promotes growth, interest rates must be higher than inflation. (If I lent out money at a 5 percent annual interest rate, but inflation was at 10 percent, I would never lend money.) Thus, the Federal Reserve watches inflation closely as part of its role of setting interest rates.

Lenders issuing long-term loans such as mortgages can also issue what are called floating rate (or adjustable) loans, whose yield depends on an interest rate (like the prime rate) which adjusts to account for changes in inflation. Using floating rates, lenders can be protected from inflation.

At the same time, some amount of inflation (usually around 1 to 2 percent) is a sign of a healthy economy. If the economy is healthy and the stock market is growing, consumer spending increases. This means that people are buying more goods, and by consequence, more goods are in demand. No inflation means that you do not have a robust economy – that there is no competitive demand for goods.

Either way, inflation must be watched closely. From basic microeconomics we know that if the demand rises because of higher personal income, the new equilibrium price is higher. Once prices rise, supply rises more (sellers of goods enter the market to take advantage of the opportunity (i.e., growth in macroeconomic terms). Hence, prices reach a new equilibrium above the previous equilibrium. Trends can theoretically spiral upward, as increased supply indicating a healthy economy further boosts the demand and supply. As an aside, this has always been Federal Reserve Chairman Alan Greenspan's major concern with an "irrationally exuberant" stock market – that the economy will overheat as a result and inflation will spiral out of control.

Effect of Inflation on Bond Prices

The effect of inflation on bond prices is very simple: when inflation goes up, interest rates rise. And when interest rates rise, bond prices fall. Therefore, when inflation goes up, bond prices fall.

The ways in which economic events, inflation, interest rates, and bond prices interact are basic to an understanding of finance – these relationships are sure to be tested in finance interviews. In general, a positive economic event (such as a decrease in unemployment, greater consumer confidence, higher personal income, etc.) drives up inflation over the long term (because there are more people working, there is more money to be spent), which drives up interest rates, which causes a decrease in bond prices.

The following table summarizes this relationship with a variety of economic events.

Economic Event	Inflation	Interest Rates	Bond Prices
Unemployment figures low	Up	Up	Down
Dollar weakens against Yen	Up	Up	Down
Consumer confidence low	Down	Down	Up
Stock Market drops	Down	Down	Up
Companies report healthy earnings	Up	Up	Down

Leading Economic Indicators

The following table is a look at leading economic indicators, and whether their rise or fall signal positive economic events or negative economic events. For finance interviews, know this chart cold.

Indicator	Positive Economic Event	Negative Economic Event
GDP	Up	Down
Unemployment	Down	Up
Inflation	Down	Up
Consumer Price Index	Down	Up
Interest Rate	Down	Up
New Home Sales	Up	Down
Existing Home Sales	Up	Down

Questions

1. What is the relationship between a bond's price and its yield?

They are inversely related. That is, if a bond's price rises, it's yield falls, and vice versa. Simply put, current yield = interest paid annually / market price * 100%.

2. How are bonds priced?

Bonds are priced based on the net present value of all future cash flows expected from the bond.

Visit the Vault Finance Career Channel at **www.vault.com/finance** — with insider firm profiles, message boards, the Vault Finance Job Board and more.

VAULT CAREER LIBRARY   93

3. How would you value a perpetual bond that pays you $1,000 a year in coupon?

Divide the coupon by the current interest rate. For example, a corporate bond with an interest rate of 10 percent that pays $1,000 a year in coupons forever would be worth $10,000.

4. When should a company issue debt instead of issuing equity?

First, a company needs a steady cash flow before it can consider issuing debt (otherwise, it can quickly fall behind interest payments and eventually see its assets seized). Once a company can issue debt, it should almost always prefer issuing debt to issuing equity.

Generally, if the expected return on equity is higher than the expected return on debt, a company will issue debt. For example, say a company believes that projects completed with the $1 million raised through either an equity or debt offering will increase its market value from $4 million to $10 million. It also knows that the same amount could be raised by issuing a $1 million bond that requires $300,000 in interest payments over its life. If the company issues equity, it will have to sell 20 percent of the company, or $1 million/$5 million ($5 million is the new value of the company after the capital infusion). This would then grow to 20 percent of $10 million, or $2 million. Thus, issuing the equity will cost the company $1 million ($2 million - $1 million). The debt, on the other hand, will only cost $300,000. The company will therefore choose to issue debt in this case, as the debt is cheaper than the equity.

Also, interest payments on bonds are tax deductible. A company may also wish to issue debt if it has taxable income and can benefit from tax shields.

Finally, issuing debt sends a quieter message to the market regarding a company's cash sitation.

5. What major factors affect the yield on a corporate bond?

The short answer: 1) interest rates on comparable U.S. Treasury bonds, and 2) the company's credit risk. A more elaborate answer would include a discussion of the fact that corporate bond yields trade at a premium, or spread, over the interest rate on comparable U.S. Treasury bonds. (For example, a five-year corporate bond that trades at a premium of 0.5 percent, or 50 basis points, over the five-year Treasury note is priced at 50 over.) The size of this spread depends on the company's credit risk: the riskier the company, the higher the interest rate the company must pay to convince investors to lend it money and, therefore, the wider the spread over U.S. Treasuries.

6. If you believe interest rates will fall, which should you buy: a 10-year coupon bond or a 10-year zero coupon bond?

The 10-year zero coupon bond. A zero coupon bond is more sensitive to changes in interest rates than an equivalent coupon bond, so its price will increase more if interest rates fall.

7. Which is riskier: a 30-year coupon bond or a 30-year zero coupon bond?

A 30-year zero coupon bond. Here's why: A coupon bond pays interest semi-annually, then pays the principal when the bond matures (after 30 years, in this case). A zero coupon bond pays no interest, but pays one lump sum upon maturity (after 30 years, in this case). The coupon bond is less risky because you receive some of your money back before over time, whereas with a zero coupon bond you must wait 30 years to receive any money back. (Another answer: The zero coupon bond is more risky because its price is more sensitive to changes in interest rates.)

8. What is The Long Bond trading at?

The Long Bond is the U.S. Treasury's 30-year bond. This question is particularly relevant for sales and trading positions, but also for corporate finance positions, as interviewers want to see that you're interested in the financial markets and follow them daily.

9. If the price of the 10-year Treasury note rises, does the note's yield rise, fall or stay the same?

Since bond yields move in the opposite direction of bond prices, if the price of a 10-year note rises, its yield will fall.

10. If you believe interest rates will fall, should you buy bonds or sell bonds?

Since bond prices rise when interest rates fall, you should buy bonds.

11. How many basis points equal .5 percent?

Bond yields are measured in basis points, which are 1/100 of 1 percent. 1 percent = 100 basis points. Therefore, .5 percent = 50 basis points.

Visit the Vault Finance Career Channel at **www.vault.com/finance** — with
insider firm profiles, message boards, the Vault Finance Job Board and more.
   VAULT CAREER LIBRARY   **95**

12. Why can inflation hurt creditors?

Think of it this way: If you are a creditor lending out money at a fixed rate, inflation cuts into the percentage that you are actually making. If you lend out money at 7 percent a year, and inflation is 5 percent, you are only really clearing 2 percent.

13. How would the following scenario affect the interest rates: the President is impeached and convicted.

While it can't be said for certain, chances are that these kind of events will lead to fears that the economy will go into recession, so the Fed would want to balance those fears by lowering interest rates to expand the economy.

14. What does the government do when there is a fear of hyperinflation?

The government has fiscal and monetary policies it can use in order to control hyperinflation. The monetary policies (the Fed's use of interest rates, reserve requirements, etc.) are discussed in detail in this chapter. The fiscal policies include the use of taxation and government spending to regulate the aggregate level of economic activity. Increasing taxes and decreasing government spending slows down growth in the economy and fights inflation.

15. Where do you think the U.S. economy will go over the next year?

Talking about the U.S. economy encompasses a lot of topics: the stock market, consumer spending, unemployment, to name a few. Underlying all these topics is the way interest rates, inflation, and bonds interact. Make sure you can speak articulately about relevant concepts discussed in this chapter when forming a view on the U.S. economic future.

16. How would you value a perpetual zero coupon bond?

The value will be zero. A zero coupon doesn't pay any coupons, and if that continues on perpetually, when do you get paid? Never – so it ain't worth nothing!

17. Let's say a report released today showed that inflation last month was very low. However, bond prices closed lower. Why might this happen?

Bond prices are based on expectations of future inflation. In this case, you can assume that traders expect future inflation to be higher (regardless of the report on last month's inflation figures) and therefore they bid bond prices down today. (A report which showed that inflation last month was benign would benefit bond prices only to the extent that traders believed it was an indication of low future inflation as well.)

18. If the stock market falls, what would you expect to happen to bond prices, and interest rates?

You would expect that bond prices would increase and interest rates would fall.

19. If unemployment is low, what happens to inflation, interest rates, and bond prices?

Inflation goes up, interest rates also increase, and bond prices decrease.

20. What is a bond's "Yield to Maturity"?

A bond's yield to maturity is the yield that would be realized through coupon and principal payments if the bond were to be held to the maturity date. If the yield is greater than the current yield (the coupon/price), it is said to be selling at a discount. If the yield is less than the current yield, it is said to be selling at a premium.

10. What do you think the Fed will do with interest rates over the next 2 years?

This question is particularly relevant in 2004, when the fed funds rate has hit an all-time low. As the economy recovers, one can reasonably expect that the fed will raise the rate slowly to stunt inflation by taking money out of the overall money supply. Presumably, the increase in production as the economy gets better will make up for the tightening policy. However, there is no right answer to this question. If you think the economy will not get better, you can easily make a case that the fed wont raise rates. However, be prepared to back up your answer either way.

CURRENCIES

A Remedial Lesson

In this global economy, an understanding of how currencies interact and what influences currency rates is vital for those interested in finance careers. The strength and stability of currencies influence trade and foreign investment. Why did so many U.S. investment banks suffer when Asian currencies plummeted in recent years? What does a strong dollar mean? When a company makes foreign investments or does business in foreign countries, how is it affected by the exchange rates among currencies? These are all issues that you'll need to know as you advance in your finance career.

To begin our discussion of currencies, let's look at some of the major terms used to discuss currencies:

Spot exchange rate: The price of one currency relative to another, i.e., the number of one currency you can buy using another currency. (The exchange rate people commonly talk about is actually the spot exchange rate.)

Example: Let's say that today the spot rate of U.S. dollars to the British pound is $1.5628/£1. If you go to the bank today, and present a teller with $1,562.80, you will receive £1,000.

Forward exchange rate: The prices of currencies at which they can be bought and sold for future delivery.

Example: Let's say that today the one-month forward rate for British pound is $1.5629, the three-month rate is $1.5625, and the one-year rate is $1.5619. These represent the prices at which the market (buyers and sellers) would agree (today) to exchange currencies one month, three months, or a year from now.

In this example, the dollar is said to be trading at a one-month forward discount, because you can get fewer pounds for the dollar in the future than you can today. Alternately, the dollar is trading at a forward premium for a three-month or one-year period, because you can get more pounds for the dollar in the future than you can today.

Exchange Rates

So what determines the rate at which dollars and pounds, or dollars and baht, or baht and roubles are exchanged? The perfect market exchange rate between two currencies is determined primarily by two factors: the interest rates in the two countries and the rates of inflation in the two countries. However, in the real world, governments of many countries regulate the exchange rate to control growth and investment of foreign capital in the economy. Economists believe that such artificial controls are the main reason currencies fall so drastically sometimes (such as the 1997-98 collapse of the Russian rouble and many Asian currencies).

Strong/weak currencies: When a currency is strong, that means its value is rising relative to other currencies. This is also called currency appreciation. When a currency is weak, its value is falling relative to other currencies. This is also called currency depreciation.

Example: *Let's say the dollar-pound exchange rate on January 1 is $1.50/£1. Three months later, on March 1, the exchange rate is $1.60/£1. The dollar has weakened, or depreciated against the pound, because it takes more dollars to equal one pound.*

Influence of Interest Rates on Foreign Exchange

The foreign exchange rate between two currencies is related to the interest rates in the two countries. If the interest rate of a foreign country relative to the home country goes up, the home currency weakens. In other words, it takes more of the home currency to buy the same amount of foreign currency. (Note: We are talking here about the real interest rate, or the interest rate after inflation. After all, if interests rates and inflation were to go up by the same amount, the effect on the country's currency would generally be a wash, of no net effect.)

Example: *Let's say the risk-free interest rate in the U.S. is 5 percent; and in the U.K. it is 10 percent. Let's also assume that the exchange rate today is $1.5/£1. If the U.K. interest rate rises to 12 percent, the British pound will tend to strengthen against the dollar.*

Explanation: When interest rates in a country rise, investments held in that country's currency (for example, bank deposits, bonds, CDs, etc.) will earn a higher rate of return. Therefore, when a country's interest rates rise, money and investments will tend to flow to that country, driving up the value of its currency. (The reverse is true when a country's interest rates fall.)

Influence of Inflation on Foreign Exchange

If the inflation in the foreign country goes up relative to the home currency, the foreign currency devalues or weakens relative to the home currency. In other words, it takes less of the home currency to buy the same amount of foreign currency.

Example: Let us say that at the beginning of the year, silver costs $1,500/lb in the U.S. and £1,000/lb in the U.K. At the same time it takes $1.5 to buy £1. Let us now assume that inflation in the U.K. is at 10 percent while that in the U.S. is at 0 percent. At the end of the year, the silver still costs $1,500/lb in the U.S., but it costs pounds £1,100 in U.K. because of inflation. Because of the U.K.'s higher inflation rate, the British pound will weaken relative to the dollar (so that, for example, it may take $1.36 to buy £1).

Advanced Explanation: Let's say again that at the beginning of the year, silver costs $1,500/lb in the U.S. and £1,000/lb in the U.K. At the same time, it takes $1.5 to buy £1. Let us now assume that inflation in the U.K. is at 10 percent while inflation in the U.S. is at 0 percent.

At the end of the year, the silver still costs $1,500/lb in the U.S., but it costs £1,100/lb in the U.K. because of inflation. If the exchange rate were to remain the same, people would start buying silver in the U.S., selling it in the U.K., and converting their money back to dollars, thus making a tidy profit. In other words, if you had $1,500, you would buy a pound of silver in U.S., sell it in the U.K. for £1,100 at the end of the year, convert the British pounds into dollars at $1.5/£1, thus receiving $1,650. For each pound of silver with which you did this, you would make a neat profit of $150. If you were to do that with a billion dollars worth of silver, you could pay for the travel expenses and buy homes in London and New York. You would have been able to take advantage of the inflation in the U.K. and created an arbitrage opportunity.

In the real world, this does not happen. If there is inflation in the U.K., the value of the pound will weaken. This is given by the relationship below.

$$\frac{f\$/£}{s\$/£} = \frac{(1 + i\$)}{(1 + i£)}$$

Here:

i\$ = the inflation in \$

i£ = the inflation in £

f\$ = the forward rate

s\$ = the spot rate

Capital Market Equilibrium

The principle of capital market equilibrium (CME) states that there should be equilibrium in the currency markets all over the world so that there is no arbitrage opportunity in shifting between two currencies. For example, if you could buy 1 pound for every 1.5 dollars, and 60 Indian rupees for every pound, you should only be able to buy a dollar for every 40 rupees.

$$\frac{Rs60}{£1} \times \frac{£1}{\$1.5} = \frac{Rs40}{\$1}$$

Consider what would happen if this was not the case. Say the dollar/pound exchange rate was \$2/£1 instead of \$1.5/£1, but the rupee/dollar and Rupee/pound relationships remained the same (1\$/40 Rs and £1/60 Rs)? You could take \$100, convert it into 4,000 rupees, take those rupees and convert it into pounds 66.67, and finally, take those 66.67 pounds and convert that back into \$133.3. You could sit at home and churn out millions of dollars this way!

Step 1: Convert dollars to rupees

$$\$100 \times \frac{Rs40}{\$1} = 4{,}000 \text{ Rs}$$

Step 2: Convert rupees to pounds

$$4{,}000 \text{ Rs} \times \frac{£1}{60 \text{ Rs}} = £66.67$$

Step 3: Convert pounds to dollars

$$£66.67 \times \frac{\$2}{£1} = \$133.33$$

Visit the Vault Finance Career Channel at **www.vault.com/finance** — with insider firm profiles, message boards, the Vault Finance Job Board and more.

VAULT CAREER LIBRARY   **103**

The three factors

These three factors – interest rates, inflation, and the principle of capital market equilibrium – govern the valuation of various currencies. Because the U.S. dollar is generally considered the world's most stable currency, it is the widely accepted basis for foreign exchange valuation. Other currencies that are considered stable are the Japanese yen and the Euro. The relative movements of these currencies, as well as others, are monitored daily.

Exchange Rate Effects on Earnings

Companies that do business abroad are exposed to currency risk. For example, if a U.S. company that manufactures goods in the U.S. sells them in England, its quarterly earnings will fluctuate based on fluctuating dollar-pound exchange rates.

If the dollar weakens (i.e., one dollar can buy fewer pounds), the company's earnings will increase because when the pounds earned by selling the product are sent back to the U.S., they will be able to buy more dollars. If the dollar strengthens, then the earnings will go down. It is important to note that there are several complex accounting rules that govern how these earnings are accounted for. Let's look at another example.

Example: If Coca-Cola sells soda in the U.K. for £1 per 2-liter bottle, and the dollar-pound exchange rate is $1.50/£1, Coca-Cola really gets $1.50 per 2-liter bottle it sells in England. If the dollar weakens, so that the exchange rate is $1.60/£1, Coca-Cola will in fact get $1.60 per pound and its earnings will be positively impacted (all else being equal).

The following table summarizes the effect of exchange rates on multinational companies.

Economic Event	Effect on Earnings of U.S. Multinational Companies	Inflation	Interest Rates
U.S. Dollar Strengthens	Negative	Falls	Fall
U.S. Dollar Weakens	Positive	Rises	Rise

Effect of Exchange Rates on Interest Rates and Inflation

A weak dollar means that the prices of imported goods will rise when measured in U.S. dollars (i.e., it will take more dollars to buy the same good). When the prices of imported goods rise, this contributes to higher inflation, which also raises interest rates. Conversely, a strong dollar means that the prices of imported goods will fall, which will lower inflation (which will lower interest rates). The following table summarizes the relationship between interest rates, inflation, and exchange rates.

Economic Event	Effect on Dollar
U.S. (Real) Interest Rates Rise	Strengthens
U.S. (Real) Interest Rates Fall	Weakens
U.S. Inflation Rates Rise	Weakens
U.S. Inflation Rates Fall	Strengthens

A note on devaluation

Under a fixed-exchange-rate system in which exchange rates are changed only by official government action, a weakening of the currency is called devaluation. To take a recent example, devaluation is what occurred in Indonesia in 1998. The Indonesian government had pegged its currency, the rupiah, to the American dollar in an attempt to artificially maintain its strength. As this policy became untenable, the government devalued its currency, causing foreign investment to flee the country and throwing the country's economy into turmoil. A strengthening of the currency under fixed exchange rates is called revaluation, rather than appreciation. These terms can be summarized in the following chart.

Type of exchange rate system	Home currency strengthens	Home currency weakens
Flexible	Appreciation	Depreciation
Fixed	Revaluation	Devaluation

Questions

1. What is the currency risk for a company like Microsoft? What about Ford?

Microsoft and Ford have different currency risks. Let's take Microsoft first. Its currency risks are created by its sales in foreign countries. For example, if it markets a software program for 100 RMB in China, and the dollar strengthens against the RMB (and the company doesn't change its price), Microsoft will be making less in U.S. dollars than it had previously anticipated. (Of course, it can react by changing its prices.)

Now let's examine Ford's currency risks. Like Microsoft, Ford is vulnerable to currency risks because it sells products in foreign currencies. In addition, the auto giant is vulnerable because it manufactures cars overseas. Let's say the company has manufacturing operations in Mexico, where cars are built, and later sold in the U.S. The cost of those operations will be sensitive to the price of the peso relative to the dollar. If the peso weakens, Ford can make its cars cheaper, sell them for lower prices, and thus gain a competitive advantage. But the opposite is also true. If the peso strengthens, Ford's labor costs will shoot up. In contrast, Microsoft doesn't have manufacturing costs overseas (most of its production costs are spent in Redmond rather than at cheaper production facilities overseas). Ford's currency risk is further complicated because some of its major competitors are in countries outside the U.S. For example, the price of the mark and the yen influences the prices at which German and Japanese competitors sell their cars. Thus Ford has greater currency risk than Microsoft.

2. When the currencies in countries like Thailand, Indonesia, and Russia fell drastically in 1998, why were U.S. and European-based investment banks hurt so badly?

I-banks were hurt on trading losses in Asia and Russia. If banks held either currency or bonds in the currencies that dropped, these assets suddenly turned non-performing, in other words, essentially worthless. (In fact, Russia's government defaulted on its government-backed bonds, so firms weren't just hurt by dropping currencies but also by loan defaults.)

3. If the U.S. dollar weakens, should interest rates generally rise, fall or stay the same?

Rise. A weak dollar means that the prices of imported goods will rise when measured in U.S. dollars (i.e., it will take more dollars to buy the same good). Rising prices of imported goods contributes to higher inflation, which raises interest rates.

4. If U.S. inflation rates fall, what will happen to the relative strength of the dollar?

It will strengthen.

5. If the interest rate in Brazil increases relative to the interest rate in the U.S., what will happen to the exchange rate between the Brazilian real and the U.S. dollar?

The real will strengthen relative to the dollar.

6. If inflation rates in the U.S. fall relative to the inflation rate in Russia, what will happen to the exchange rate between the dollar and the rouble?

The dollar will strengthen relative to the rouble.

7. What is the difference between currency devaluation and currency depreciation?

Devaluation occurs in a fixed-exchange-rate system and is usually fixed as a function of governement policy, while depreciation occurs when a country allows its currency to move according to the international currency exchange market.

8. What is the effect on U.S. multinational companies if the U.S. dollar strengthens?

U.S. multinationals see their earnings decrease when the dollar strengthens. Essentially, sales in foreign currencies don't amount to as many U.S. dollars when the dollar strengthens.

9. What are some of the main factors that govern foreign exchange rates?

Chiefly: interest rates, inflation, and capital market equilibrium.

Visit the Vault Finance Career Channel at **www.vault.com/finance** — with
insider firm profiles, message boards, the Vault Finance Job Board and more.
VAULT CAREER LIBRARY   **107**

10. If the spot exchange rate of dollars to pounds is \$1.60/£1, and the one-year forward rate is \$1.50/£1, would we say the dollar is forecast to be strong or weak relative to the pound?

The forward exchange rate indicates the rate at which traders are willing to exchange currencies in the future. In this case, they believe that the dollar will strengthen against the pound in the coming year (that one dollar will be able to buy more pounds one year from now than it can now).

OPTIONS AND DERIVATIVES

The Wild West of Finance

Derivatives aren't the most trusted of financial instruments. They received some bad press in the mid-1990s when Bankers Trust, the leading marketer of derivatives, was accused by several of its key clients, including Procter & Gamble and Gibson Greetings, of misinforming them about the risk of its derivatives instruments. The trustworthiness of derivatives wasn't helped any when Bankers Trust bankers, which had a reputation for being high-flying risk-takers, were caught on tape making dismissive comments about whether their clients would be able to understand what they were doing or had done wrong. Derivatives received another black mark for their role in the bankruptcy of Orange County, California, the largest municipal bankruptcy in U.S. history. In a case similar to the Bankers Trust case, Orange County officials charged that they had been misled about the risk of their investments, which involved complex derivatives. To settle that suit, the county's lead investment banker, Merrill Lynch, agreed to pay $437.1 million.

In 2003, Warren Buffet, one of the most successful investors of all time, spoke out against derivates, stating, "[I] view them as time bombs, both for the parties that deal in them and the economic system."

What are these scary things called derivatives? Quite simply, derivatives are financial instruments that derive their value out of or have their value contingent upon the values of other assets like stocks, bonds, commodity prices or market index values.

Derivatives are often used to hedge financial positions. Hedging is a financial strategy designed to reduce risk by balancing a position in the market. Often, hedges work like insurance: a small position pays off large amounts if the price of a certain security reaches a certain price. On other occasions, derivatives are used to hedge positions by locking in prices.

Options

We'll begin our discussion with a look at options, the most common derivative. Options, as the word suggests, give the bearers the "option" to buy or sell a security – without the obligation to do so. Two of the simplest forms of options are call options and put options.

Call options

A call option gives the holder the right to purchase an asset for a specified price on or before a specified expiration date. (Technically, this definition refers to an "American option." Standard European call options can only be converted on the expiration date. For simplicity's sake, our examples will assume the call options are American.) The specified price is called the "exercise price" or "strike price." Let's take a look at an example. A July 1 call option on IBM stock has an exercise price of $70. The owner of this option is entitled to purchase IBM stock at $70 at anytime up to and including the expiration date of July 1. If in June, the price of IBM stock jumps up to $80, the holder can exercise the option to buy stock from the option seller for $70. The holder can then turn around and sell it to the market for $80 and make a neat profit of $10 per share (minus the price of the option, which we will discuss later). Or the holder can hold onto the number of shares purchased through the option.

Note: When a call option's exercise price is exactly equal to the current stock price, the option is called an "at the money" call. When a call option has an exercise price that is less than the current stock price, it is called an "in the money" call. When a call option's exercise price is greater than the current stock price, it is called an "out of the money" call.

Put options

The other common form of option is a put option. A put option gives its holder the right to sell an asset for a specified exercise price on or before a specified expiration date. (Again, options in Europe can be exercised only on the expiration date.) For example, a July 1 put option on IBM with an exercise price of $70 entitles its owner to sell IBM stock at $70 at any time before it expires in July, even if market price is lower than $70. So if the price drops to $60, the holder of the put option would buy the stock at $60, sell it for $70 by exercising her option, and make a neat profit of $10 (minus the price of the option). On the other hand, if the price goes over $70, the holder of the put option will not exercise the option and will lose the amount he paid to buy the option.

Writing Options

Sounds pretty neat, eh? But how are these options created? And who buys and sells the stock that the options give holders the right to buy and sell?

Well, there is an entire market – called the options market – that helps these transactions go through. For every option holder there must be an option seller. This seller is often referred to as the writer of the option. So selling a put option is called writing a put. Anyone who owns the underlying asset, such as an individual or a mutual fund – can write options.

Let's go back to our previous example. If you buy the July 1 call option on IBM stock with an exercise price of $70, you are betting that the price of IBM will go above $70 before July 1. You can make this bet only if there is someone who believes that the price of IBM will not go above $70 before July 1. That person is the seller, or "writer," of the call option. He or she first gets a non-refundable fee for selling the option, which you pay. If the price goes to $80 in June and you exercise your option, the person who sold the call option has to buy the stock from the market at $80 (assuming he does not already own it) and sell it to you at $70, thus incurring a loss of $10.

But remember that you had to buy the option originally. The seller of the option, who has just incurred a loss of $10, already received the price of the option when you bought the option. On the other hand, say the price had stayed below $70 and closed at $60 on June 30. The seller would have made the amount he sold the option for, but would not make the difference between the $70 strike price and the $60 June 30 closing price. Why not? Because as the buyer of the call option, you have the right to buy at $70 but is not obligated to. If the stock price of IBM stays below $70, you as the option buyer will not exercise the option.

Note: If the writer of the call option already owns IBM stock, he is essentially selling you his upside on his IBM stock, or the right to all gains above $70. Obviously, he doesn't think it's very likely that IBM will rise above $70 and he hopes to simply pocket the option price.

Summary options chart

	Action to take
Person believes a stock will go up	Buy a call
	Write a put
Person believes a stock will go down	Buy a put
	Write a call

Options Pricing

Understanding how an option writer makes money brings up the natural question: How does an option get priced?

There are at least six factors that affect the value of an option: the stock price, exercise price, the volatility of the stock price, the time to expiration, the interest rate and the dividend rate of the stock. To understand how these factors affect option values, we will look at their effect on call options (the option to buy a security).

• **Price of underlying security:** If an option is purchased at a fixed exercise price, and the price of the underlying stock increases, the value of a call option increases. Clearly, if you have the option to buy IBM stock at $100, the value of your option will increase with any increase in stock price: from $95 to $100, from $100 to $105, from $105 to $106, etc. (The value of a put option in this scenario decreases.)

• **Exercise ("strike") price:** Call options can be bought at various exercise prices. For example, you can buy an option to buy stock in IBM at $100, or you can buy an option to buy stock in IBM at $110. The higher the exercise price, the lower the value of the call option, as the stock price has to go up higher for you to be in the money. (Here, the value of the put option increases, as the stock price does not need to fall as low.)

• **Volatility of underlying security:** The option value increases if the volatility of the underlying stock increases. Let's compare similar options on a volatile Internet stock like Google and a more steady stock like Wal-Mart. Say that the Google stock price has been fluctuating from $70 to $130 in the last three months. Let's also say that Wal-Mart has been fluctuating from $90 to $110. Now let's compare call options with an exercise price of $100 and a time until expiration of three months.

Although the average price for both stocks in the past three months has been $100, you would value the option to buy Google stock more because there is a greater possibility that it will increase well above $100. (Perhaps Google would rise to $130, rather than Wal-Mart's $110, if the previous three months were replicated.) The reason this potential upside increases the option's value is that the downside loss that you can incur is fixed. You have the option to exercise and not the obligation to buy at $100. No matter how low Google's stock might go, the most you would lose is the cost of the option. Volatility increases the value of both call and put options.

- **Time to expiration:**. The more time the holder has to exercise the option, the more valuable the option. This makes common sense. The further away the exercise date, the more time for unpredictable things to happen and the broader the range of likely stock price increases. Moreover, the more time the option holder has, the lower the present value of the exercise price will be (thus increasing the option value). Like volatility, time to expiration increases the value of both put and call options.

- **Interest rates:** If interest rates are higher, the exercise price has a lower present value. This also increases the value of the call option.

- **Dividends:** A higher dividend rate policy of the company means that out of the total expected return on the stock, some is being delivered in the form of dividends. This means that the expected capital gain of the stock will be lower, and the potential increase in stock price will be lower. Hence, larger dividend pay outs lower the call value.

The following table summarizes the relationships between these factors and the value of options:

If this variable increases	The value of a call option
Stock price	Increases
Exercise price	Decreases
Volatility	Increases
Time to expiration	Increases
Interest rate	Increases
Dividend payouts	Decreases

In the end, the price of an option, like any security, is determined by the market. However, as with the various valuation techniques for companies discussed previously, there are standard methods of pricing options, most prominently the Black-Scholes model. This model has essentially become the industry standard, and is a fairly good predictor of how the market prices options.

Those interviewing for jobs as derivative traders should consult a finance textbook and understand the model in further detail, as interviewers for these position are bound to ask more detailed questions based on the Black-Scholes model and its application. Other popular derivatives instruments include forwards, futures, and swaps.

Forwards

A forward contract is an agreement that calls for future delivery of an asset at an agreed-upon price. Let's say a farmer grows a single crop, wheat. The revenue from the entire planting season depends critically on the highly volatile price of wheat. The farmer can't easily diversify his position because virtually his entire wealth is tied up in the crop. The miller who must purchase wheat for processing faces a portfolio problem that is a mirror image of the farmer's. He is subject to profit uncertainty because of the unpredictable future of the wheat price when the day comes for him to buy his wheat.

Both parties can reduce their risk if they enter into a forward contract requiring the farmer to deliver the wheat at a previously agreed upon price, regardless of what the market price is at harvest time. No money needs to change hands at the time the agreement is made. A forward contract is simply a deferred delivery sale of some asset with an agreed-upon sales price. The contract is designed to protect each party from future price fluctuations. These forwards are generally used by large companies that deal with immense quantities of commodities, like Cargill or Archer Daniels Midland.

Futures

The futures contract is a type of forward that calls for the delivery of an asset or its cash value at a specified delivery or maturity date for an agreed upon price. This price is called the futures price, and is to be paid when the contract matures. The trader who commits to purchasing the commodity on the delivery date is said to be in the long position. The trader who takes the short position commits to delivering the commodity when the contract matures.

Futures differ from other forwards in the fact that they are liquid, standardized, traded on an exchange, and their prices are settled at the end of each trading day (that is, the futures traders collect/pay their day's gains and losses at the end of each day). Futures are actively traded and liquid securities. For example, for agricultural commodities, the exchange sets allowable grades of a commodity (for example, No. 2 hard winter wheat or No. 1 soft red wheat). The place or means of delivery of the commodity is specified as issued by approved warehouses. The dates of delivery are also standardized. The prices of the major agricultural futures appear in *The Wall Street Journal*. Futures are also available on other commodities, like gold and oil.

Swaps

Another derivative, a swap, is a simple exchange of future cash flows. Some popular forms of swaps include foreign exchange swaps and interest rate swaps. Let's first examine foreign exchange swaps.

Say Sun Microsystems outsources its software development to India on a regular basis. In such a situation, it would make payments to the firms in India in rupees, thus find itself exposed to foreign exchange rate fluctuation risks. To hedge these exchange risks, Sun would want to enter into a foreign exchange swap – a predetermined exchange of currency – with another party. For example, Sun might want to swap $1.0 million for Rs 40 million for each of the next five years. For instance, it could enter into a swap with the Birla Group in India, which has many expenses in U.S. dollars and is thus also subject to the same exchange rate fluctuation risk. By agreeing to a foreign exchange swap, both companies protect their business from exchange rate risks.

Interest rate swaps work similarly. Consider a firm (Company A) that has issued bonds (which, remember, means essentially that it has taken loans) with a total par value of $10 million at a fixed interest rate of 8 percent. By issuing the bonds, the firm is obligated to pay a fixed interest rate of $800,000 at the end of each year. In a situation like this, it can enter into an interest rate swap with another party (Company B), where Company A pays Company B the LIBOR rate (a floating, or variable, short-term interest rate measure) and Company B agrees to pay Company A the fixed rate. In such a case, Company A would receive $800,000 each year that it could use to make its loan payment. For its part, Company A would be obligated to pay $10 million x LIBOR each year to Company B. Hence Company A has swapped its fixed interest rate debt to a floating rate debt. (The company swaps rates with Company B, called the counterparty. The counterparty gains because presumably it wants to swap its floating rate debt for fixed rate debt, thus locking in a fixed rate.) The chart below illustrates this swap.

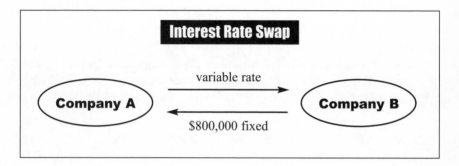

Questions

1. When would you write a call option on Disney stock?

When you expect the price of Disney stock to fall (or stay the same). Because a call option on a stock is a bet that the value of the stock will increase, you would be willing to write (sell) a call option on Disney stock to an investor if you believed Disney stock would not rise. (In this case, the profit you would make would be equal to the option premium you received when you sold the option.)

2. Explain how a swap works.

A swap is an exchange of future cash flows. The most popular forms include foreign exchange swaps and interest rate swaps. They are used to hedge volatile rates, such as currency exchange rates or interest rates.

3. Say I hold a put option on Microsoft stock with an exercise price of $60, the expiration date is today, and Microsoft is trading at $50. About how much is my put worth, and why?

Your put is worth about $10, because today, you can sell a share of stock for $60, and buy it for $50. (If the expiration date were in the future, the option would be more valuable, because the stock could conceivably drop more.)

4. When would a trader seeking profit from a long-term possession of a future be in the long position?

The trader in the long position is committed to buying a commodity on a delivery date. She would hold this position if she believes the commodity price will increase.

5. All else being equal, which would be less valuable: a December put option on Amazon.com stock or a December put option on Bell Atlantic stock?

The put option on Bell Atlantic should be less valuable. Amazon.com is a more volatile stock, and the more volatile the underlying asset, the more valuable the option.

6. All else being equal, which would be more valuable: a December call option for eBay or a January call option for eBay?

The January option: The later an option's expiration date, the more valuable the option.

7. Why do interest rates matter when figuring the price of options?

Because of the ever-important concept of net present value, all else being equal, higher interest rates lower the value of call options.

8. If the strike price on a put option is below the current price, is the option holder at the money, in the money or out of the money?

Because a put option gives the holder the right to sell a security at a certain price, the fact that the strike (or exercise) price is below the current price would mean that the option holder would lose money. Translate that knowledge into option lingo, and you know that the option holder is out of the money.

9. If the current price of a stock is above the strike price of a call option, is the option holder at the money, in the money, or out of the money?

Because a call option gives the holder the right to buy a security, the holder in this scenario is in the money (making money).

10. When would you buy a put option on General Mills stock?

Because buying a put option gives you the option to sell the stock at a certain price, you would do this if you expect the price of General Mills stock to fall.

11. What is the main difference between futures contracts and forward contracts?

The main difference between forward and futures contracts is that futures contracts are traded on exchanges and forwards are traded over-the-counter. Because of this distinction, you can only trade specific futures contracts that are traded on the exchange. Forward contracts are more flexible because they are privately negotiated, and can represent any assets and can change settlement dates should both parties agree.

Competition on the Street – and beyond – is heating up. With the finance job market tightening, you need to be your best.

We know the finance industry. And we've got experts that know the finance environment standing by to review your resume and give you the boost you need to snare the financial position you deserve.

Finance Resume Writing and Resume Reviews

- Have your resume reviewed by a practicing finance professional.

- For resume writing, start with an e-mailed history and 1- to 2-hour phone discussion. Our experts will write a first draft, and deliver a final draft after feedback and discussion.

- For resume reviews, get an in-depth, detailed critique and rewrite within TWO BUSINESS DAYS.

Finance Career Coaching

Have a pressing finance career situation you need Vault's expert advice with? We've got experts who can help.

- Trying to get into investment banking from business school or other careers?

- Switching from one finance sector to another – for example, from commercial banking to investment banking?

- Trying to figure out the cultural fit of the finance firm you should work for?

"Thank you, thank you, thank you! I would have never come up with these changes on my own!"

– W.B., Associate, Investment Banking, NY

"Having an experienced pair of eyes looking at the resume made more of a difference than I thought."

– R.T., Managing Director, SF

"I found the coaching so helpful I made three appointments!"

– S.B., Financial Planner, NY

For more information go to www.vault.com/finance

V∆ULT
> the most trusted name in career information™

MERGERS & ACQUISITIONS

Why Merge?

When two companies decided to combine forces in a blockbuster merger, the news dominates financial headlines. Why are companies in industries ranging from telecommunications to financial services to retail looking to merge? Because of the much referred to "synergies" that theoretically result from a merger. Because of synergies, the combination of the two companies that merge are thought to be greater than the sum of the two independently. Examples of these synergies include: reductions in redundant workforce, and utilizing the technology, market share of the other party to the deal, and combinations of service offerings. Let's take a look at the major reasons for M&A activity.

One important reason that a company might merge with another company is to gain a foothold into a new market, which can come in the form of a product or a geographic region, and sometimes both. For example, in the January 2004 JPMorgan Chase/Bank One merger, JPMorgan not only added to its already strong investment and commercial banking activities but also gained a strong consumer banking franchise in Bank One, thus boosting its ability to compete in the consumer market with perennial powerhouse Citigroup. Prior to the merger, most of Bank One's 1,800 consumer branches were located in the South and the Midwest, while JPMorgan had a stronghold in New York and Texas. After the combination, the firm had some 2,300 branches in 17 states, with very little overlap.

In other cases, companies merge to enter new geographic markets. Chrysler sold its cars almost exclusively in North America; Daimler-Benz was strong in Europe. Thus the two agreed to combine and form DaimlerChrysler.

Sometimes mergers are driven by the coveted brand recognition of the acquisition. For example, by acquiring US Robotics, 3Com added US Robotics' strong brand recognition in the modem industry. (That merger also added an important hardware strength to 3Com's drive to challenge Cisco as the computer networking leader.)

In other cases, companies merge to consolidate operations, thus lowering costs and boosting profits (think economies of scale). Why pay for two legal departments, two PR departments, or two headquarters when you only need one? Moreover, if a company can buy 10,000 sheets of metal for less than it can buy 5,000, it might consider merging with someone who could give it that advantage.

And sometimes, companies merge just to get bigger in a consolidating industry. In some industries, most notably banking and brokerage, executives believe that size is required in order to compete as the industry consolidates around a handful of major players. Size certainly played a part in the JPMorgan/Bank One combo, as it boosted JPMorgan's assets to $1.1 billion, rivaling Citigroup's $1.2 billion. Similarly, Bank of America's October 2003 acquisition of FleetBoston Financial made BofA the ninth largest asset manager in the U.S., up from the No. 17 spot it held prior to the merger.

Why Not Merge?

While mergers are fun and exciting to talk about, the post-merger logistics aren't always as sexy. Did you know that more than one out of every five mergers does not achieve the synergies initially targeted? This isn't just because of poor implementation after the merger. Many mergers are simply ill-advised or involve a clash of corporate cultures.

So why do failed mergers go through? One reason is that many mergers are also the result of management egos and the excitement generated in a merger mania market. For example, the recent Mobil/Exxon deal was constructed largely in private through the efforts of the CEOs of the two companies, Lucio Noto of Mobil and Lee Raymond of Exxon. (This is not to say that this merger will not work, but to simply note that it, like many mergers, was driven by the personalities and choices of individuals.)

Another powerful force pushing mergers are the huge I-banking fees that the deals generate. Investment bankers are going to argue to their clients that the mergers are in their best interest because they are in fact in their (the bankers') best interest. Goldman Sachs and Credit Suisse First Boston both pocketed about $30 million from their advisory roles in the AT&T/TCI merger. Think they didn't have some incentive to be enthusiastic when talking about telecom/cable TV synergy?

Types of buyers

There are two main categories of buyers of companies: **strategic buyers** and **financial buyers**. Strategic buyers are corporations who want to acquire another company for strategic business reasons. Financial buyers are buyers who want to acquire another company purely as a financial investment.

Financial buyers are typically LBO (Leveraged Buyout) Funds or other private equity funds.

Who will pay more for a company: strategic buyers or financial buyers? Nine times out of ten, a strategic buyer will pay more than a financial buyer. In addition to the company's existing revenues and cash flow, strategic buyers also hope (though they are often wrong) that they will be able to grow the company's cash flows faster by expanding into complementary markets, reducing overlapping costs, etc. As a result, the strategic buyer will assume that the company's post-acquisition cash flows will be higher than are currently expected to be. When they discount these higher cash flows, they will get a higher valuation.

Valuing a company for strategic and financial buyers

When you prepare a valuation analysis for a strategic buyer, your projected cash flows will be different (that is, higher) than the cash flows for the company as a "stand alone" entity. You will prepare a "pro forma" financial model that typically assumes faster revenue growth and reduction of certain costs because the acquiring company will be able to derive strategic efficiencies from the acquired company.

Conversely, a valuation analysis for financial buyer cannot take into account these synergies. At most you may be able to do a valuation model that assumes benefits to the financial buyer such as tax benefits from interest payments on debt used to acquire the company, and perhaps some lower costs if there are "obvious" cost savings and efficiencies the financial buyer can force on the target company once the acquisition is complete.

Stock Swaps vs. Cash Offers

Bankers and finance officials at companies have a couple of financing options when they consider how to structure a merger: a stock swap or a cash deal.

Stock swaps occur more often when there is a strong stock market, because companies with a high market capitalization can acquire companies with that more valuable stock. In 1998, when the equity markets were peaking, 67 percent of the merger activity in 1998 was accomplished through stock, versus 33 percent through cash, according to *Fortune* magazine. In 1988, the ratio was only 7 percent stock to 93 percent cash. Of course, the volatility of the stock market can make stock swaps tricky. We should understand why many announced mergers become pending once the stock market crashes – the initial assumptions for valuing the companies are not true anymore when the market falls. Interestingly, when the market is strong, the merger mania heightens. Even though valuations are inflated, the environment is optimistic and it looks like both companies made off well – the acquired company is given a very high market value, while the acquirer appears to have gained valuable assets.

In a cash deal, shareholders must pay taxes when they receive the cash. The tax rate for their earnings is at the ordinary income marginal tax rate (your tax rate increases as the income bracket you are in goes higher), which is 39.6 percent for wealthy individuals. By contrast, in a stock swap, no taxes are paid at the time of the swap. But when the swapped stock is sold in the market, the shareholder must pay capital gains tax at a marginal tax rate of 20 percent. The U.S. government sets tax laws this way as a part of its fiscal strategy to regulate the amount of cash in the economy and to control factors like inflation.

Type of Merger	1988	1998
Stock	7%	67%
Cash	93%	33%

Source: Fortune

Tender Offers

Tender offers are associated with hostile takeovers. In a tender offer, the hostile acquirer renders a tender offer for the public's stock at a price higer than the current market in an attempt to gather a controlling interest in (majority ownership of) a company. For example, let's say Mr. T-Bone Pickins wants to take over Acme Internet Corp., and that Acme stock is trading at $20 per share. Say Pickins issues an advertisement to the public – usually through the newspaper, or sometimes through direct mail campaigns – that announces that he will buy Acme stock for $40 a share (double the going market price). If he can garner 51 percent of the stock outstanding through this method, he will also have gained controlling ownership of the stock.

When a tender offer is issued, the share price rises close to the offering price – in our example, to $40 per share. The proximity to the actual tender offer is dependent on the likelihood the offer will succeed. (If the share price didn't rise, I, as T-Bone Pickins, would simply buy from the market rather than following though with the tender offer, wouldn't I? Or better still, if the stock price didn't rise, I, as John Doe investor, would simply buy from the market and sell to T-Bone.)

However, Pickins doesn't have to buy all the stock offered to him through a tender offer. If he receives offers for more than 75 percent of the stock and doesn't want to buy more than 51 percent, he can buy 2/3 of the stock that each shareholder offers him. For example, if you were an Acme shareholder interested in T-Bone's offer, and were willing to sell him your 1,000 shares, he would only buy 2/3 of your stock (666 shares) for $40 and the other 1/3 for $20. (The consequence of this, of course, is that you would only sell him 2/3 of your shares.) Also, because he has made a tender offer, if Pickins does not receive offers to buy 51 percent at his price, he does not have to purchase the shares offered to him.

Why would anyone offer $40 a share to buy a company that the market valued at only $20 a share? Basically, if they believe they can do substantially better with the company than current management – whether because of expected synergies with companies they already own, a belief that the company is inefficient and mismanaged, a belief the company is worth more in parts than as a whole, or any other reason they believe the company's inherent assets to be substantially more valuable than its current market value. (All the reasons together result in the control premium, or the premium over the current value.)

Of course, the target company can defend itself. Say Acme's management hires Goldman Sachs to make a counter bid to prevent a hostile takeover and offers another tender at an even higher price. Sometimes this leads to an auction situation (the famous RJR Nabisco case is an example of an escalating auction, although no tenders were involved there).

Mergers vs. Acquisitions

The terms merger and acquisition are often used loosely and interchangeably. For example, a bit of tension arose in the Bankers Trust/Deutsche Bank deal when Deutsche Bank officials became irked at Bankers Trust execs' continual referral to the deal as a merger when it was in fact an acquisition. When two companies of relatively equal size decide to combine forces, it is referred to as a merger of equals. Examples of this type of deal are the recent Sears/Kmart merger or the Sprint/Nextel merger. On the other hand, if one company buys out another, the deal is considered a purchase or acquisition. Examples of this include JPMorgan Chase's acquisition of Bank One or Oracle's acquisition of Peoplesoft.

Despite this sometimes loose definition of how we normally categorize mergers and acquisitions, there are real legal and accounting differences between the two – which, it ends up, basically depend on the method used for the transaction (stock swap, etc. as discussed above).

Will That Be Cash or Stock?

The choice of whether to make a cash deal or stock swap depends largely on the tax factors discussed above. However, it can also depend on other factors. For example, if the stockholders of the company being acquired value the stock of their acquirer and believe that the merged company will be a long-term industry leader (and is thus a company whose stock they would like to receive), they will push for a stock swap. The volatility of the stock market must also be considered; if the market is behaving like a roller coaster, a company's board of directors and shareholders may feel they can not stomach a stock swap, and opt for a cash deal. Another factor that may come into play is how soon an acquired company will receive cash in a cash deal, and how badly it needs the cash. If we remember our discussion of net present value, we know that cash today is worth more than cash tomorrow.

Visit the Vault Finance Career Channel at **www.vault.com/finance** — with
insider firm profiles, message boards, the Vault Finance Job Board and more.

VAULT CAREER LIBRARY   127

Accretive vs. Dilutive Mergers

A merger can be either accretive or dilutive. A merger is accretive when the acquiring company's earnings per share will increase after the merger. A merger is dilutive when the acquiring company's earnings will fall after a merger.

Let's take a look at an example. Say a shoe company, Big Gun, wants to acquire a fast growing competitor, Ubershoe. Also suppose that Big Gun's earnings are $10 million, that it has 1 million outstanding shares (and thus has earnings of $10 per share), and that Ubershoe's earnings are $2 million.

Whether the acquisition will be accretive or dilutive depends on the amount Big Gun will pay for Ubershoe. Say that Big Gun agrees to a stock swap in which it issues 500,000 shares which it will trade for all of Ubershoe's shares. The combined company will have 1.5 million shares and $12 million in earnings. The new earnings per share are $8 per share. This deal is dilutive to Big Gun's earnings.

But say that the terms of the acquisition are different, and Big Gun agrees to issue 100,000 new shares of stock instead of 500,000. The combined company will have $12 million in earnings and 1.1 million shares, or earnings of $10.91 per share. This deal is accretive to Big Gun's earnings.

Figuring out whether a merger is accretive or dilutive can be accomplished by adding up the companies' earnings and shares (as we have done in this case), but an easier way is to use the companies' price to earnings ratios (P/Es). The rule is as follows: When a company with a higher price to earnings ratio (we'll call the company "Company 1," and label it's P/E ratio "P/E1") acquires a firm, "Company 2" of a lower P/E ratio (which we will label P/E2), it is an accretive merger.

If Company 1 acquires Company 2

Earnings Relationship	Merger Type
$P/E_1 > P/E_2$	Accretive
$P/E_1 < P/E_2$	Dilutive

Questions

1. Describe a recent M&A transaction that you've read about.

If you are preparing for an I-banking interview, this is a must-prepare question. Read the papers or search the Internet and have at least one transaction thoroughly prepared. You should be able to cover various aspects of the transactions. You should know what the structure of the transaction was and who was buying whom.

For example, you could talk about the Sears/Kmart merger announced in late 2004. That cash and stock transaction was worth an estimated $11 billion. Although the deal was advertised as a merger of equals and the Sears name will remain, by the structure of the deal, it's clear that Kmart acted as an acquirer. Sears shareholders were offered the choice between $50 in cash or half of one share of Sears Holdings, the new parent company, which was valued at $50.61. Kmart shareholders received one share of Sears Holding for each of their shares, which closed the day before the deal was announced at $101.22. To purchase the larger and more established Sears, Kmart used the strong gains in its stock during the previous year and half leading up to the deal, plus its almost $3 billion in excess cash. At the time of the announcement, Sears and Kmart said they expect cost savings and increased sales of $500 million a year, after the merger is completed.

2. What were the reasons behind an M&A transaction you've read about? Does that transaction make sense?

Perhaps more important than understanding the mechanics of transactions is understanding the factors that drive M&A activity. The Sears/Kmart deal, for example, brought together two giant and struggling companies in hopes that, combined, they'll be able to better compete with other leading retailers such as Wal-Mart, Target and Home Depot.

The Sears/Kmart deal created the third largest retailer in the country, behind Wal-Mart and Home Depot. Kmart was strong in clothing and home accessories and recently added name brands such as Thalia Sodi, Jaclyn Smith, Joe Boxer and Martha Stewart Everyday. Sears, meanwhile, was known for its appliances and tools, specifically for its Kenmore and Craftsmen brands. The combined firm hopes to blend both of the firms' strong suits, offering quality appliances and tools (and a reputation for good service) to Kmart shoppers, and discount clothing and low prices to Sears customers. The increased shopping convenience is expected to allow the

Visit the Vault Finance Career Channel at www.vault.com/finance — with insider firm profiles, message boards, the Vault Finance Job Board and more.

VAULT CAREER LIBRARY   129

combined firm to formidably battle against Wal-Mart, Home Depot and Target, which lost its No. 3 retiler standing as a result of the deal.

Again, your interviewer will expect you to discuss both the financial structure of a deal, its impact on earnings, as well as its strategic drivers.

3. Your client is a privately held human resources software company. You are advising the company in the potential sale of the company. Who would you expect to pay more for the company: Oracle Software (a competitor), or Kohlberg Kravis Roberts (an LBO fund)?

Oracle. A strategic buyer like Oracle would typically pay more than a financial buyer like KKR. Oracle would be able to derive additional benefits and therefore higher cash flows from the purchase than would KKR. For example, Oracle would be able to cut support and administrative staff, combine the company's R&D budget with Oracle's, get lower costs on supplies and manufacturing in larger volumes, etc.

4. Are most mergers stock swaps or cash transactions and why?

In strong markets, most mergers are stock swaps, largely because the stock prices of companies are so high.

5. What is a dilutive merger?

A merger in which the acquiring company's earnings per share decreases as a result of the merger. Also remember the P/E rule: A dilutive merger happens when a company with a lower P/E ratio acquires a company with a higher P/E ratio.

6. What is an accretive merger?

The type of merger in which the acquiring company's earnings per share increase. With regard to P/E ratio, this happens when a company with a higher P/E ratio acquires a company with a lower P/E ratio. The acquiring company's earnings per share should rise following the merger.

7. Company A is considering acquiring Company B. Company A's P/E ratio is 55 times earnings, whereas Company B's P/E ratio is 30 times earnings. After Company A acquires Company B, will Company A's earnings per share rise, fall, or stay the same?

Company A's earnings per share will rise, because of the following rule: When a higher P/E company buys a lower P/E company, the acquirer's earnings-per-share will rise. The deal is said to be accretive, as opposed to dilutive, to the acquirer's earnings.

8. Can you name two companies that you think should merge?

Identifying synergies between two companies is only part of correctly answering this question. You also need to ensure that the merger will not raise antitrust issues with FTC. For example, you could say that Apple and Microsoft should merge, but the combined company will have an unfair monopoly on the operating system market and the FTC will not approve the merger. (Moreover, the people running the two companies don't like each other and would not want to merge.)

9. What is a hostile tender offer?

If company A wants to acquire company B, but company B refuses, company A can issue a tender offering. In this offer, company A will take advertisements in major newspapers like *The Wall Street Journal* to buy stock in company B at a price much above the market price. If company A is able to get more than 50 percent of the stock that way, it can officially run and make all major decisions for company B – including firing the top management. This is something of a simplistic view; there are scores of rules and regulations from the SEC governing such activity.

10. What is a leveraged buyout? How is it different than a merger?

A leveraged buyout occurs when a group, by refinancing a company with debt, is able to increase the valuation of the company. LBOs are typically accomplished by either financial groups such as KKR or company management, whereas M&A deals are led by companies in the industry.

11. If Company A buys Company B, what will the Balance Sheet of the combined company look like?

In this accounting, simply add each line item on the Balance Sheet.

BRAINTEASERS AND GUESSTIMATES

Stress Tests

Perhaps even more so than tough finance questions, brainteasers and guesstimates can unnerve the most icy-veined, well-prepared finance candidate. Even if you know the relationships between inflation, bond prices and interest rates like the back of a dollar bill, all your studying may not help you when your interviewer asks you how many ping pong balls fit in a 747.

That is partly their purpose. Investment bankers and other finance professionals need to be able to work well under pressure, so many interviewers believe that throwing a brainteaser or guesstimate at a candidate is a good way to test an applicant's battle-worthiness. But these questions serve another purpose, too – interviewers want you to showcase your ability to analyze a situation, and to form conclusions about this situation. It is not necessarily important that you come up with a correct answer, just that you display strong analytical ability

Acing Guesstimates

We'll start by discussing guesstimates, for which candidates are asked to come up with a figure, usually the size of a market or the number of objects in an area. Although guesstimates are more commonly given in interviews for consulting positions, they do pop up in finance interviews as well. Practicing guesstimates is a good way to begin preparing for stress questions in finance interviews, as they force candidates to think aloud – precisely what interviewers want to see. The most important thing to remember about brainteasers, guesstimates, or even simple math questions that are designed to be stressful is to let your interviewer see how your mind works.

The best approach for a guesstimate question is to think of a funnel. You begin by thinking broadly, then slowly narrowing down the situation towards the answer. Let's look at this approach in context. Let's go back to the question of how many ping pong balls fit in a 747. The first thing you need to determine is the volume of the ping pong ball and the volume of a 747.

For any guesstimate or brainteaser question, you will need to understand whether your interviewer will be providing any direction or whether you will have to make assumptions. Therefore, begin the analysis of a guesstimate or brainteaser question with a question to your interviewer, such as, "What is the volume of a single ping pong ball?" If the interviewer does not know or refuses to provide any answer, then you must assume the answer. If they do provide the information, you may ask a series of follow-up questions. For this example, let's assume your interviewer wants you to make the assumptions. Your answer might go something like this:

Let's assume that the volume of a ping pong ball is three cubic inches. Now let's assume that all the seats in the plane are removed. I know that an average refrigerator is about 23 cubic feet, and you could probably fit two average people in the space occupied by that refrigerator, so let's say that the volume of an average person is 12 cubic feet, or 20,736 cubic inches

Okay, so a 747 has about 400 seats in it, excluding the galleys, lavatories, and aisles on the lower deck and about 25 seats on the upper deck. Let's assume there are three galleys, 14 lavatories, and three aisles (two on the lower deck and one on the upper deck) and that the space occupied by the galleys is a six-person equivalent, by the lavatories is a two-person equivalent, and the aisles are a 50-person equivalent on the lower deck and a 20-person equivalent on the upper deck. That's an additional 18, 28, and 120 person-volumes for the remaining space. We won't include the cockpit since someone has to fly the plane. So there are about 600 person-equivalents available.

In addition to the human volume, we have to take into account all the cargo and extra space – the belly holds, the overhead luggage compartments, and the space over the passengers' heads. Let's assume the plane holds four times the amount of extra space as it does people, so that would mean extra space is 2,400 person-equivalents in volume. (Obviously, this assumption is the most important factor in this guesstimate. Remember that it's not important that this assumption be correct, just that you know the assumption should be made.)

Therefore, in total we have 3,000 (or 600 + 2,400) person-equivalents in volume available. 3,000 x 20,736 cubic inches means we have 62,208,000 cubic inches of space available (we can round to 60 million). At three cubic inches per ball, a 747 could hold about 20 million balls. However, spheres do not fit perfectly together. Eliminate a certain percentage – spheres lose about 30 percent when packed – and cut your answer to about 14 million.

You might be wondering how you would calculate all these numbers in your head! No one expects you to be a human calculator, so you should be writing down these numbers as you develop them. Then you can do the math on paper, in front of the interviewer, which will further demonstrate your analytical abilities.

Visit the Vault Finance Career Channel at **www.vault.com/finance** — with insider firm profiles, message boards, the Vault Finance Job Board and more.

VAULT CAREER LIBRARY   **135**

You choose the numbers, so pick nice round numbers that are easy for you to manipulate. Even if you just read a study that states that there are 270 million people in the United States, no interviewer will flinch if you estimate the number of Americans as 300 million.

Note: The extra step

Don't forget to add the "extra step" that often pop into guesstimates. In our previous example, this step involved reducing our estimate of ping pong balls because spheres do not pack perfectly together. If you're trying to figure out how many blocks there are in New York City, remember to eliminate blocks covered by Central Park (and other parks). If you're determining the number of black cars in the United States, once you've estimated the number of cars in America, make sure you estimate what percentage of them are black.

Brainteasers

Now we'll turn our attention to brainteasers, which are often used in finance interviews. Some of these, like the legendary, "Why is the manhole round?" question which reportedly originated at Microsoft, have no definite answer. Others do have answers, but even with these, interviewers are more interested in assessing creativity, composure, and your ability to deconstruct a problem and ask directed and relevant questions.

Remember, brainteasers are very unstructured, so it is tough to suggest a step-by-step methodology. However, there are a couple of set rules. First, take notes as your interviewer gives you a brainteaser, especially if it's heavy on math. Second, think aloud so your interviewer can hear your thought process. This may seem unnatural at first; the examples at the end of this chapter will show you how to logically attack these questions, and how you should vocalize your analysis. In addition to the riddle-type brainteasers, finance interviewers will often throw out simple mathematical questions designed to see how quick thinking you are. The math questions are most often given to analyst applicants. The best way to prepare for these questions (other than to find out which of these questions are most common, which we've happily done for you), is simply to know that you might get one of them. That way, if you do get one, you won't be quite as surprised or unprepared.

Questions

1. How many gallons of white house paint are sold in the U.S. every year?

THE "START BIG" APPROACH: If you're not sure where to begin, start with the basic assumption that there are 270 million people in the U.S. (or 25 million businesses, depending on the question). If there are 270 million people in the United States, perhaps half of them live in houses (or 135 million people). The average family size is about three people, so there would be 45 million houses in the United States. Let's add another 10 percent to that for second houses and houses used for other purposes besides residential. So there are about 50 million houses.

If houses are painted every 10 years, on average (notice how we deftly make that number easy to work with), then there are 5 million houses painted every year. Assuming that one gallon of paint covers 100 square feet of wall, and that the average house has 2,000 square feet of wall to cover, then each house needs 20 gallons of paint. So 100 million gallons of paint are sold per year (5 million houses x 20 gallons). (Note: If you want to be fancy, you can ask your interviewer whether you should include inner walls as well.) If 80 percent of all houses are white, then 80 million gallons of white house paint are sold each year. (Don't forget that last step!)

THE "START SMALL" APPROACH: Take a town of 27,000 (about 1/10,000 of the population). If you use the same assumption that half the town lives in houses in groups of three, then there are 4,500 houses, plus another 10 percent, which makes 5,000 houses. Painted every 10 years, 500 houses are being painted in any given year. If each house has 2,000 square feet of wall, and each gallon of paint covers 100 square feet, then each house needs 20 gallons – so 10,000 gallons of house paint are sold each year in your typical town. Perhaps 8,000 of those are white. Multiply by 10,000 you have 80 million gallons.

Your interviewer may then ask you how you would get an actual number, on the job. Use your creativity – contacting major paint producers would be smart, putting in a call to HUD's statistics arm could help, or even conducting a small sample of the second calculation in a few representative towns is possible.

2. What is the size of the market for disposable diapers in China?

Here's a good example of a market sizing. How many people live in China? A billion. Because the population of China is young, a full 600 million of those inhabitants might be of child-bearing age. Half are women, so there are about 300 million Chinese women of childbearing age. Now, the average family size in China is restricted, so it might be 1.5 children, on average, per family. Let's say two-thirds of Chinese women have children. That means that there are about 300 million children in China. How many of those kids are under the age of two? About a tenth, or 30 million. So there are at least 30 million possible consumers of disposable diapers.

To summarize:

1 billion people x 60% childbearing age = 600,000,000 people

600,000,000 people x 1/2 are women = 300,000,000 women of childbearing age

300,000,000 women x 2/3 have children = 200,000,000 women with children

200,000,000 women x 1.5 children each = 300,000,000 children

300,000,000 children x 1/10 under age 2 = 30 million

3. How many square feet of pizza are eaten in the United States each month?

Take your figure of 300 million people in America. How many people eat pizza? Let's say 200 million. Now let's say the average pizza-eating person eats pizza twice a month, and eats two slices at a time. That's four slices a month. If the average slice of pizza is perhaps six inches at the base and 10 inches long, then the slice is 30 square inches of pizza. So four pizza slices would be 120 square inches. Since one square foot equals 144 square inches, let's assume that each person who eat pizza eats one square foot per month. Since there are 200 million pizza-eating Americans, 200 million square feet of pizza are consumed in the US each month.

To summarize:

300 million people in America

200 million eat pizza

Average slice of pizza is six inches at the base and 10 inches long = 30 square inches (height x half the base)

Average American eats four slices of pizza a month

Four pieces x 30 square inches = 120 square inches (one square foot is 144square inches), so let's assume one square foot per person

1 square foot x 200 million people = 200 million square feet a month

4. How would you estimate the weight of the Chrysler building?

This is a process guesstimate – the interviewer wants to know if you know what questions to ask. First, you would find out the dimensions of the building (height, weight, depth). This will allow you to determine the volume of the building. Does it taper at the top? (Yes.) Then, you need to estimate the composition of the Chrysler building. Is it mostly steel? Concrete? How much would those components weigh per square inch? Remember the extra step – find out whether you're considering the building totally empty or with office furniture, people, etc.? (If you're including the contents, you might have to add 20 percent or so to the building's weight.)

5. Why are manhole covers round?

The classic brainteaser, straight to you via Microsoft (the originator). Even though this question has been around for years, interviewees still encounter it.

Here's how to "solve" this brainteaser. Remember to speak and reason out loud while solving this brainteaser!

Why are manhole covers round? Could there be a structural reason? Why aren't manhole covers square? It would make it harder to fit with a cover. You'd have to rotate it exactly the right way. So many manhole covers are round because they don't need to be rotated. There are no corners to deal with. Also, a round manhole cover won't fall into a hole because it was rotated the wrong way, so it's safer.

Looking at this, it seems corners are a problem. You can't cut yourself on a round manhole cover. And because it's round, it can be more easily transported. One person can roll it.

6. If you look at a clock and the time is 3:15, what is the angle between the hour and the minute hands?

The answer to this is not zero! The hour hand, remember, moves as well. The hour hand moves a quarter of the way between three and four, so it moves a

Visit the Vault Finance Career Channel at **www.vault.com/finance** — with insider firm profiles, message boards, the Vault Finance Job Board and more.

VAULT CAREER LIBRARY   **139**

quarter of a twelfth (1/48) of 360 degrees. So the answer is seven and a half degrees, to be exact.

7. You have a five-gallon jug and a three-gallon jug. You must obtain exactly four gallons of water. How will you do it?

You should find this brainteaser fairly simple. If you were to think out loud, you might begin by examining the ways in which combinations of five and three can come up to be four. For example: (5 - 3) + (5 - 3) = 4. This path does not actually lead to the right answer, but it is a fruitful way to begin thinking about the question. Here's the solution: fill the three-gallon jug with water and pour it into the five-gallon jug. Repeat. Because you can only put two more gallons into the five-gallon jug, one gallon will be left over in the three-gallon jug. Empty out the five-gallon jug and pour in the one gallon. Now just fill the three-gallon jug again and pour it into the five-gallon jug. (Mathematically, this can be represented 3 + 3 - 5 + 3 = 4)

8. You have 12 balls. All of them are identical except one, which is either heavier or lighter than the rest. The odd ball is either hollow while the rest are solid, or solid while the rest are hollow. You have a scale, and are permitted three weighings. Can you identify the odd ball, and determine whether it is hollow or solid?

This is a pretty complex question, and there are actually multiple solutions. First, we'll examine what thought processes an interviewer is looking for, and then we'll discuss one solution.

Start with the simplest of observations. The number of balls you weigh against each other must be equal. Yeah, it's obvious, but why? Because if you weigh, say three balls against five, you are not receiving any information. In a problem like this, you are trying to receive as much information as possible with each weighing.

For example, one of the first mistakes people make when examining this problem is that they believe the first weighing should involve all of the balls (six against six). This weighing involves all of the balls, but what type of information does this give you? It actually gives you no new information. You already know that one of the sides will be heavier than the other, and by weighing six against six, you will simply confirm this knowledge. Still, you want to gain information about as many balls as possible (so weighing one against one is obviously not a good idea). Thus the best first weighing is four against four.

Secondly, if you think through this problem long enough, you will realize how precious the information gained from a weighing is: You need to transfer virtually every piece of information you have gained from one weighing to the next. Say you weigh four against four, and the scale balances. Lucky you! Now you know that the odd ball is one of the unweighed four. But don't give into the impulse to simply work with those balls. In this weighing, you've also learned that the eight balls on the scale are normal. Try to use this information.

Finally, remember to use your creativity. Most people who work through this problem consider only weighing a number of balls against each other, and then taking another set and weighing them, etc. This won't do. There are a number of other types of moves you can make – you can rotate the balls from one scale to another, you can switch the balls, etc.

Let's look at one solution:

For simplicity's sake, we will refer to one side of the scale as Side A, and the other as Side B.

Step 1: Weigh four balls against four others.

Case A: If, on the first weighing, the balls balance

If the balls in our first weighing balance we know the odd ball is one of those not weighed, but we don't know whether it is heavy or light. How can we gain this information easily? We can weigh them against the balls we know to be normal. So:

Step 2 (for Case A): Put three of the unweighed balls on the Side A; put three balls that are known to be normal on Side B.

I. If on this second weighing, the scale balances again, we know that the final unweighed ball is the odd one.

Step 3a (for Case A): Weigh the final unweighed ball (the odd one) against one of the normal balls. With this weighing, we determine whether the odd ball is heavy or light.

II. If on this second weighing, the scale tips to Side A, we know that the odd ball is heavy. (If it tips to Side B, we know the odd ball is light, but let's proceed with the assumption that the odd ball is heavy.) We also know that the odd ball is one of the group of three on Side A.

Visit the Vault Finance Career Channel at **www.vault.com/finance** — with insider firm profiles, message boards, the Vault Finance Job Board and more.

V/\ULT CAREER LIBRARY **141**

Step 3b (for Case A): Weigh one of the balls from the group of three against another one. If the scale balances, the ball from the group of three that was unweighed is the odd ball, and is heavy. If the scale tilts, we can identify the odd ball, because we know it is heavier than the other. (If the scale had tipped to Side B, we would use the same logical process, using the knowledge that the odd ball is light.)

Case B: If the balls do not balance on the first weighing

If the balls do not balance on the first weighing, we know that the odd ball is one of the eight balls that was weighed. We also know that the group of four unweighed balls are normal, and that one of the sides, let's say Side A, is heavier than the other (although we don't know whether the odd ball is heavy or light).

Step 2 (for Case B): Take three balls from the unweighed group and use them to replace three balls on Side A (the heavy side). Take the three balls from Side A and use them to replace three balls on Side B (which are removed from the scale).

> **I.** If the scale balances, we know that one of the balls removed from the scale was the odd one. In this case, we know that the ball is also light. We can proceed with the third weighing as described in step 3b from Case A.

> **II.** If the scale tilts to the other side, so that Side B is now the heavy side, we know that one of the three balls moved from Side A to Side B is the odd ball, and that it is heavy. We proceed with the third weighing as described in step 3b in Case A.

> **III.** If the scale remains the same, we know that one of the two balls on the scale that was not shifted in our second weighing is the odd ball. We also know that the unmoved ball from Side A is heavier than the unmoved ball on Side B (though we don't know whether the odd ball is heavy or light).

Step 3 (for Case B): Weigh the ball from Side A against a normal ball. If the scale balances, the ball from Side B is the odd one, and is light. If the scale does not balance, the ball from Side A is the odd one, and is heavy.

As you can see from this solution, one of the keys to this problem is understanding that information can be gained about balls even if they are not being weighed. For example, if we know that one of the balls of two groups that are being weighed is the odd ball, we know that the unweighed balls are normal. Once this is known, we realize that breaking the balls up into smaller and smaller groups of three (usually eventually down to three balls), is a good strategy – and an ultimately successful one.

9. You are faced with two doors. One door leads to your job offer (that's the one you want!), and the other leads to the exit. In front of each door is a guard. One guard always tells the truth. The other always lies. You can ask one question to decide which door is the correct one. What will you ask?

The way to logically attack this question is to ask how you can construct a question that provides the same answer (either a true statement or a lie), no matter who you ask.

There are two simple answers. Ask a guard: "If I were to ask you if this door were the correct one, what would you say?" The truthful guard would answer yes (if it's the correct one), or no (if it's not). Now take the lying guard. If you asked the liar if the correct door is the right way, he would answer no. But if you ask him: "If I were to ask you if this door were the correct one, what would you say," he would be forced to lie about how he would answer, and say yes. Alternately, ask a guard: "If I were to ask the other guard which way is correct, what would he say?" Here, the truthful guard would tell you the wrong way (because he is truthfully reporting what the liar would say), while the lying guard would also tell you the wrong way (because he is lying about what the truthful guard would say).

If you want to think of this question more mathematically, think of lying as represented by -1, and telling the truth as represented by +1. The first solution provides you with a consistently truthful answer because $(-1)(-1) = 1$, while $(1)(1) = 1$. The second solution provides you with a consistently false answer because $(1)(-1) = -1$, and $(-1)(1) = -1$.

10. A company has 10 machines that produce gold coins. One of the machines is producing coins that are a gram light. How do you tell which machine is making the defective coins with only one weighing?

Think this through – clearly, every machine will have to produce a sample coin or coins, and you must weigh all these coins together. How can you somehow indicate which coins came from which machine? The best way to do it is to have every machine crank a different number of coins, so that machine 1 will make one coin, machine 2 will make two coins, and so on. Take all the coins, weigh them together, and consider their weight against the total theoretical weight. If you're four grams short, for example, you'll know that machine 4 is defective.

11. The four members of U2 (Bono, the Edge, Larry and Adam) need to get across a narrow bridge to play a concert. Since it's dark, a flashlight is required to cross, but the band has only one flashlight, and only two people can cross the bridge at a time. (This is not to say, of course, that if one of the members of the band has crossed the bridge, he can't come back by himself with the flashlight.) Adam takes only a minute to get across, Larry takes two minutes, the Edge takes five minutes, and slowpoke Bono takes 10 minutes. A pair can only go as fast as the slowest member. They have 17 minutes to get across. How should they do it?

The key to attacking this question is to understand that Bono and the Edge are major liabilities and must be grouped together. In other words, if you sent them across separately, you'd already be using 15 minutes. This won't do. What does this mean? That Bono and the Edge must go across together. But they can not be the first pair (or one of them will have to transport the flashlight back).

Instead, you send Larry and Adam over first, taking two minutes. Adam comes back, taking another minute, for a total of three minutes. Bono and the Edge then go over, taking 10 minutes, and bringing the total to 13. Larry comes back, taking another two minutes, for a total of 15. Adam and Larry go back over, bringing the total time to 17 minutes.

12. What is the decimal equivalent of 3/16 and 7/16?

A commonly-used Wall Street interview question, this one isn't just an attempt to stress you out or see how quick your mind works. This question also has practical banking applications. Stocks often are traded at prices reported in 1/16s of a dollar. If you don't know the answer off the top of your head, an easy way to start is with what you do know. You know $\frac{1}{4}$ = .25, so dividing each side by 2, 1/8 = .125 and 1/16 = .0625. Just multiple that to get what you're looking for, so 3/16 = .1875 and 7/16 = .4375.

13. What is the sum of the numbers from one to 50?

Another question that recent analyst hires often report receiving. This is a relatively easy one: pair up the numbers into groups of 51 (1 + 50 = 51; 2 + 49 = 51; etc.). Twenty-five pairs of 51 equals 1275.

14. You have a painting that was $320 which is now selling for 20 percent off. How much is the discounted price?

Calculate quickly: What's 80 percent of $320? The answer is $256. Even in a question like this, if you are good with numbers and use shortcuts, don't be afraid to talk aloud. For example: 80 percent of $320 can be broken down to a calculation like 80 percent of $80 x $4, or $256.

15. How many Delta Airlines planes will take off in the next hour in United States?

There are several ways to attack this question. One way is to start by figuring out the number of airports in the United States. Most states have one or two large airports from which a major carrier departs. So on average, you can assume that there are 1.2 large airports per state. Finally, if you say that one Delta plane departs every 10 minutes, you can see that there 6 take off per hour from each airport, so you can estimate that there are

1.2 x 50 x 6, or 360 Delta planes taking off this hour.

16. A straight flush beats a four-of-a-kind in poker because it is more unlikely. But think about how many straight flushes there are – if you don't count wraparound straights, you can have a straight flush starting on any card from two to 10 in any suit (nine per suit). That means there are 36 straight flushes possible. But how many four of a kinds are there – only 13. What's wrong with this reasoning?

Immediately, you should think about the difference between a straight flush and a four-of-a-kind. One involves five cards, and the other involves four. Intuitively, that's what should strike you as the problem with the line of reasoning. Look closer and you'll see what that means: for every four of a kind, there are actually a whole bunch of five-card hands: 48 (52 - 4) in fact. There are actually 624 (48 x 13) of them in all.

17. If you have seven white socks and nine black socks in a drawer, how many do you have to pull out blindly in order to ensure that you have a matching pair?

Three. Let's see – if the first one is one color, and the second one is the other color, the third one, no matter what the color, will make a matching pair. Sometimes you're not supposed to think that hard.

Visit the Vault Finance Career Channel at **www.vault.com/finance** — with insider firm profiles, message boards, the Vault Finance Job Board and more.

VAULT CAREER LIBRARY   **145**

18. Tell me a good joke that is neither sexist nor racist.

Have a few good, tasteful jokes ready.

19. If I were to fill this room with pennies, how many pennies would fit in?

A literally in-your-face guesstimate.

20. Say you are driving two miles on a one-mile track. You do one lap at 30 miles an hour. How fast do you have to go to average 60 miles an hour?

This is something of a trick question, and was recently received by a Goldman candidate. The first thought of many people is to say 90 miles an hour, but consider: If you have done a lap at 30 miles an hour, you have already taken two minutes. Two minutes is the total amount of time you would have to take in order to average 60 miles an hour. Therefore, you can not average 60 miles an hour over the two laps.

FINAL
ANALYSIS

Don't be scared off by the horror stories you may have heard about finance interviews. True, some interviewers will get tough – don't be shocked if you encounter a few screamers, rapid-fire math questions or questions designed to catch you off guard – just remember most people are just trying to get to know you. They want to find out if you can handle the job, if you're interested in finance and if you're the kind of person they want to have around the office, especially if you have to pull an all-nighter. Remember to study the relevant finance topics. If you're interviewing for an equity position, know what the stock market is doing. If you're auditioning for the M&A department, get to know the particulars of a deal that you've found interesting, especially if the deal was done by the firm at which you're interviewing. Overall, make sure you have a good grasp of basic finance concepts and convince your interviewer that you have the ability to learn the more complex aspects of the job.

You should also be ready for the more laid-back interviews. Be ready to talk about yourself. You'll tell them about your hobbies and interests, your experience and your education, among other things. Remember why you want to go into banking (or asset management, or venture capital, etc.) and why you're interested in that particular firm.

Overall, be confident. If you've practiced your answers and done your research, most of the questions should be answerable if you take the time to think about what they're looking for. Remember to dress and act professionally, which includes showing up on time. Good luck!

APPENDIX

Finance Glossary

Accretive merger: A merger in which the acquiring company's earnings per share increase.

Balance Sheet: One of the four basic financial statements, the Balance Sheet presents the financial position of a company at a given point in time, including Assets, Liabilities, and Equity.

Beta: A value that represents the relative volatility of a given investment with respect to the market.

Bond price: The price the bondholder (the lender) pays the bond issuer (the borrower) to hold the bond (i.e., to have a claim on the cash flows documented on the bond).

Bond spreads: The difference between the yield of a corporate bond and a U.S. Treasury security of similar time to maturity.

Buy-side: The clients of investment banks (mutual funds, pension funds and other entities often called "institutional investors") that buy the stocks, bonds and securities sold by the investment banks. (The investment banks that sell these products to investors are known as the "sell-side.")

Callable bond: A bond that can be bought back by the issuer so that it is not committed to paying large coupon payments in the future.

Call option: An option that gives the holder the right to purchase an asset for a specified price on or before a specified expiration date.

Capital Asset Pricing Model (CAPM): A model used to calculate the discount rate of a company's cash flows.

Commercial bank: A bank that lends, rather than raises money. For example, if a company wants $30 million to open a new production plant, it can approach a commercial bank like Bank of America or Citibank for a loan. (Increasingly, commercial banks are also providing investment banking services to clients.)

Commercial paper: Short-term corporate debt, typically maturing in nine months or less.

Commodities: Assets (usually agricultural products or metals) that are generally interchangeable with one another and therefore share a common price. For example, corn, wheat, and rubber generally trade at one price on commodity markets worldwide.

Common stock: Also called common equity, common stock represents an ownership interest in a company (as opposed to preferred stock, see below). The vast majority of stock traded in the markets today is common, as common stock enables investors to vote on company matters. An individual with 51 percent or more of shares owned controls a company and can appoint anyone he/she wishes to the board of directors or to the management team.

Comparable transactions (comps): A method of valuing a company for a merger or acquisition that involves studying similar transactions.

Convertible preferred stock: A type of equity issued by a company, convertible preferred stock is often issued when it cannot successfully sell either straight common stock or straight debt. Preferred stock pays a dividend, similar to how a bond pays coupon payments, but ultimately converts to common stock after a period of time. It is essentially a mix of debt and equity, and most often used as a means for a risky company to obtain capital when neither debt nor equity works.

Capital market equilibrium: The principle that there should be equilibrium in the global interest rate markets.

Convertible bonds: Bonds that can be converted into a specified number of shares of stock.

Cost of Goods Sold: The direct costs of producing merchandise. Includes costs of labor, equipment, and materials to create the finished product, for example.

Coupon payments: The payments of interest that the bond issuer makes to the bondholder.

Credit ratings: The ratings given to bonds by credit agencies. These ratings indicate the risk of default.

Currency appreciation: When a currency's value is rising relative to other currencies.

Currency depreciation: When a currency's value is falling relative to other currencies.

Currency devaluation: When a currency weakens under fixed exchange rates.

Visit the Vault Finance Career Channel at **www.vault.com/finance** — with insider firm profiles, message boards, the Vault Finance Job Board and more.

VAULT CAREER LIBRARY   **151**

Currency revaluation: When a currency strengthens under fixed exchange rates.

Default premium: The difference between the promised yields on a corporate bond and the yield on an otherwise identical government bond.

Default risk: The risk that the company issuing a bond may go bankrupt and "default" on its loans.

Derivatives: An asset whose value is derived from the price of another asset. Examples include call options, put options, futures, and interest-rate swaps.

Dilutive merger: A merger in which the acquiring company's earnings per share decrease.

Discount rate: A rate that measures the risk of an investment. It can be understood as the expected return from a project of a certain amount of risk.

Discounted Cash Flow analysis (DCF): A method of valuation that takes the net present value of the free cash flows of a company.

Dividend: A payment by a company to shareholders of its stock, usually as a way to distribute some or all of the profits to shareholders.

EBIAT: Earnings Before Interest After Taxes. Used to approximate earnings for the purposes of creating free cash flow for a discounted cash flow.

EBIT: Earnings Before Interest and Taxes.

EBITDA: Earnings Before Interest, Taxes, Depreciation and Amortization.

Enterprise Value: Levered value of the company, the Equity Value plus the market value of debt.

Equity: In short, stock. Equity means ownership in a company that is usually represented by stock.

The Fed: The Federal Reserve Board, which manages the country's economy by setting interest rates.

Fixed income: Bonds and other securities that earn a fixed rate of return. Bonds are typically issued by governments, corporations and municipalities.

Float: The number of shares available for trade in the market times the price. Generally speaking, the bigger the float, the greater the stock's liquidity.

Floating rate: An interest rate that is pegged to other rates (such as the rate paid on U.S. Treasuries), allowing the interest rate to change as market conditions change.

Forward contract: A contract that calls for future delivery of an asset at an agreed-upon price.

Forward exchange rate: The price of currencies at which they can be bought and sold for future delivery.

Forward rates (for bonds): The agreed-upon interest rates for a bond to be issued in the future.

Futures contract: A contract that calls for the delivery of an asset or its cash value at a specified delivery or maturity date for an agreed upon price. A future is a type of forward contract that is liquid, standardized, traded on an exchange, and whose prices are settled at the end of each trading day.

Glass-Steagall Act: Part of the legislation passed during the Depression (Glass-Steagall was passed in 1933) designed to help prevent future bank failure - the establishment of the F.D.I.C. was also part of this movement. The Glass-Steagall Act split America's investment banking (issuing and trading securities) operations from commercial banking (lending). For example, J.P. Morgan was forced to spin off its securities unit as Morgan Stanley. Since the late 1980s, the Federal Reserve has steadily weakened the act, allowing commercial banks to buy investment banks.

Goodwill: An account that includes intangible assets a company may have, such as brand image.

Hedge: A balance on a position in the market in order to reduce risk.

High-yield bonds (a.k.a. junk bonds): Bonds with poor credit ratings that pay a relatively high rate of interest, or can be bought for cents per dollar of face value.

Holding Period Return: The income earned over a period as a percentage of the bond price at the start of the period.

Income Statement: One of the four basic financial statements, the Income Statement presents the results of operations of a business over a specified period of time, and is composed of Revenues, Expenses, and Net Income.

Initial Public Offering (IPO): The dream of every entrepreneur, the IPO is the first time a company issues stock to the public. "Going public" means more than raising money for the company: By agreeing to take on public shareholders, a company enters a whole world of required SEC filings and quarterly revenue and earnings reports, not to mention possible shareholder lawsuits.

Investment grade bonds: Bonds with high credit ratings that pay a relatively low rate of interest, but are very low risk.

Leveraged Buyout (LBO): The buyout of a company with borrowed money, often using that company's own assets as collateral. LBOs were the order of the day in the heady 1980s, when successful LBO firms such as Kohlberg Kravis Roberts made a practice of buying companies, restructuring them, and reselling them or taking them public at a significant profit.

Liquidity: The amount of a particular stock or bond available for trading in the market. For commonly traded securities, such as large cap stocks and U.S. government bonds, they are said to be highly liquid instruments. Small cap stocks and smaller fixed income issues often are called illiquid (as they are not actively traded) and suffer a liquidity discount, i.e., they trade at lower valuations to similar, but more liquid, securities.

The Long Bond: The 30-year U.S. Treasury bond. Treasury bonds are used as the starting point for pricing many other bonds, because Treasury bonds are assumed to have zero credit risk take into account factors such as inflation. For example, a company will issue a bond that trades "40 over Treasuries." The 40 refers to 40 basis points (100 basis points = 1 percentage point).

Market Cap(italization): The total value of a company in the stock market (total shares outstanding x price per share).

Money market securities: This term is generally used to represent the market for securities maturing within one year. These include short-term CDs, Repurchase Agreements, Commercial Paper (low-risk corporate issues), among others. These are low risk, short-term securities that have yields similar to Treasuries.

Mortgage-backed bonds: Bonds collateralized by a pool of mortgages. Interest and principal payments are based on the individual homeowners making their mortgage payments. The more diverse the pool of mortgages backing the bond, the less risky they are.

Multiples method: A method of valuing a company that involves taking a multiple of an indicator such as price-to-earnings, EBITDA, or revenues.

Municipal bonds: Bonds issued by local and state governments, a.k.a., municipalities. Municipal bonds are structured as tax-free for the investor, which means investors in muni's earn interest payments without having to pay federal taxes. Sometimes investors are exempt from state and local taxes, too. Consequently, municipalities can pay lower interest rates on muni bonds than other bonds of similar risk.

Net present value (NPV): The present value of a series of cash flows generated by an investment, minus the initial investment. NPV is calculated because of the important concept that money today is worth more than the same money tomorrow.

Non-convertible preferred stock: Sometimes companies issue non-convertible preferred stock, which remains outstanding in perpetuity and trades like stocks. Utilities are the most common issuers of non-convertible preferred stock.

Par value: The amount a bond issuer will commit to pay back, the principal, when the bond expires.

P/E ratio: The price to earnings ratio. This is the ratio of a company's stock price to its earnings-per-share. The higher the P/E ratio, the faster investors believe the company will grow.

Prime rate: The average rate U.S. banks charge to companies for loans.

Put option: An option that gives the holder the right to sell an asset for a specified price on or before a specified expiration date.

Securities and Exchange Commission (SEC): A federal agency that, like the Glass-Steagall Act, was established as a result of the stock market crash of 1929 and the ensuing depression. The SEC monitors disclosure of financial information to stockholders, and protects against fraud. Publicly traded securities must first be approved by the SEC prior to trading.

Securitize: To convert an asset into a security that can then be sold to investors. Nearly any income-generating asset can be turned into a security. For example, a 20-year mortgage on a home can be packaged with other mortgages just like it, and shares in this pool of mortgages can then be sold to investors.

Selling, General & Administrative Expense (SG&A): Costs not directly involved in the production of revenues. SG&A is subtracted as part of expenses from Gross Profit to get EBIT.

Spot exchange rate: The price of currencies for immediate delivery.

Statement of Cash Flows: One of the four basic financial statements, the Statement of Cash Flows presents a detailed summary of all of the cash inflows and outflows during a specified period.

Statement of Retained Earnings: One of the four basic financial statements, the Statement of Retained Earnings is a reconciliation of the Retained Earnings account. Information such as dividends or announced income is provided in the statement. The Statement of Retained Earnings provides information about what a company's management is doing with the company's earnings.

Stock: Ownership in a company.

Stock swap: A form of M&A activity in whereby the stock of one company is exchanged for the stock of another.

Strong currency: A currency whose value is rising relative to other currencies.

Swap: A type of derivative, a swap is an exchange of future cash flows. Popular swaps include foreign exchange swaps and interest rate swaps.

10K: An annual report filed by a public company with the Securities and Exchange Commission (SEC). Includes financial information, company information, risk factors, etc.

Tender offers: A method by which a hostile acquirer renders an offer to the shareholders of a company in an attempt to gather a controlling interest in the company. Generally, the potential acquirer will offer to buy stock from shareholders at a much higher value than the market value.

Treasury securities: Securities issued by the U.S. government. These are divided into Treasury bills (maturity of up to 2 years), Treasury notes (from 2 years to 10 years maturity), and Treasury bonds (10 years to 30 years). As they are government guaranteed, often treasuries are considered risk-free. In fact, while U.S. Treasuries have no default risk, they do have interest rate risk; if rates increase, then the price of UST's will decrease.

Underwrite: Most commonly, the valuing of a pre-IPO stock performed by investment banks when they help companies issue securities to investors. Technically, the investment bank buys the securities from the company and immediately resells the securities to investors for a slightly higher price, making money on the spread.

Weak currency: A currency whose value is falling relative to other currencies.

Yield to call: The yield of a bond calculated up to the period when the bond is called (paid off by the bond issuer).

Yield: The annual return on investment. A high-yield bond, for example, pays a high rate of interest.

Yield to maturity: The measure of the average rate of return that will be earned on a bond if it is bought now and held to maturity.

Zero coupon bonds: A bond that offers no coupon or interest payments to the bondholder.

About the Authors

D. Bhatawedekhar is the pen name of an associate with one of Wall Street's bulge bracket investment banking firms. He is a graduate of the University of Chicago's Graduate School of Business, and majored in finance.

Dan Jacobson is a writer and editor who graduated with a Bachelor of Arts from Cornell University in 1997 and received his MBA from the Massachusetts Institute of Technology in 2002. Dan has worked at Merrill Lynch in its real estate principal investment group and, prior to business school, as a management consultant at PricewaterhouseCoopers.

Hussam Hamadeh is co-founder of Vault. He holds a BA in economics from UCLA and a JD/MBA from the Wharton School of Business and the University of Pennsylvania Law School, where he was an editor on Law Review. He is a member of the New York Bar and is a member of the Board of Managers of the University of Pennsylvania Law School.

Decrease your T/NJ Ratio
(Time to New Job)

Use the Internet's most targeted job search tools for finance professionals.

Vault Finance Job Board

The most comprehensive and convenient job board for finance professionals. Target your search by area of finance, function, and experience level, and find the job openings that you want. No surfing required.

VaultMatch Resume Database

Vault takes match-making to the next level: post your resume and customize your search by area of finance, experience and more. We'll match job listings with your interests and criteria and e-mail them directly to your inbox.